NORTHERN PIKE & MUSKIE

THE HUNTING & FISHING LIBRARY®

By Dick Sternberg

DICK STERNBERG is widely acclaimed for his pioneering research on the coldwater habits of large northern pike. Because of his discoveries, summertime pike location is no longer the mystery that it once was.

CY DECOSSE INCORPORATED
Chairman: Cy DeCosse
President: James B. Maus
Executive Vice President: William B. Jones

NORTHERN PIKE & MUSKIE
Author and Project Director: Dick Sternberg
Editors: Janice Cauley, Tom Carpenter
Project Manager: Joseph Cella
Senior Art Director: Bradley Springer
Art Director: Dave Schelitzche
Research and Photo Director: Eric Lindberg
Researchers: Steven Hauge, Dave Maas, Jim Moynagh
Principal Photographers: Mike Hehner, William Lindner
Photo Assistants: Steven Hauge, Dave Maas, Jim Moynagh
Staff Photographers: Mark Macemon, Mette Nielsen, Mike Parker
Director of Development, Planning and Production: Jim Bindas
Production Manager: Amelia Merz
Electronic Publishing Analyst: Joe Fahey
Senior Production Artist: Mark Jacobson
Typesetting: Linda Schloegel
Production Staff: Peter Gloege, Linda Schloegel, Nik Wogstad
Shop Supervisor: Greg Wallace
Prop Stylist: Jim Huntley
Illustrator: Thomas Boll

Primary Scientific Advisor: Dr. James Diana – University of Michigan

Contributing Photographers: Ian J. Adams; Appel Color Photography; Kim Baily; Christopher Batin; Joe Bucher; Walter Chandoha; Brian Chipman/Vermont Department of Fish & Wildlife; Michael Collier; Grand Rapids Herald-Review; Len & Betty Hartman; In-Fisherman, Inc.; Robin F. Knox/ Colorado Division of Wildlife; Rod Kuehn/University of Minnesota; Chuck Nields; Steve Payne; Larry Ramsell; Gerald S. Ratliff; Saskatchewan Economics Diversification and Trade; Wayne Shiels; Dick Sternberg; Don Wirth; Mike Woodside

Cooperating Individuals and Agencies: Andersen Sales – Tom Andersen; Jerry Anderson; Angler's All – Mike Gilmore, Roger LaPenter; Leonard Baron; Bucher Tackle Co. – Joe Bucher; Burger Bros. Sporting Goods – John Goplin; Camp Fish – Dan Craven; Canadian Consulate General – Bruce Verner; Ted Capra's Sporting Goods – Dean Capra; Clif's Wilderness Camp – Clif Santa; Paul Dechaine; Jan Eggers; Field and Stream Magazine; Fishing Hall of Fame – Bob Kutz; Grass River Lodge Ltd. – Ike Enns; Dick Grzywinski; Illinois Natural History Survey – Dave Wahl; Iowa Department of Natural Resources – Jim Christianson; John Jakobs; Jerry's Bait – Jerry & Crystal Matzen; Chris Johnson; Kentucky Department of Wildlife Resources – Daniel Brewer; Kentucky Silver Muskie Club – John Lyon; Doug Knoer; Brad Kolstad; Lake of the Woods Tourism Center – Patrick Brett; Maryland Department of Natural Resources – John Foster; Michigan Department of Natural Resources – Ned Fogle; Miner Bay Camps – Gerald Howard; Minnesota Department of Natural Resources – Bruce Gilbertson, Don Pereira, Duane Shodeen, Bob Strand, Jerry Younk; Missouri Department of Conservation – Kevin Richards; Muskie Hunter Magazine – Dan Laubenstein; Muskies, Inc.; New York Department of Environmental Conservation – Steve Mooradian; Ohio Division of Wildlife – Richard Day; Ohio Huskie Muskie Club – Mike Dudek; John Olson; Pat Olson; Ontario Federation of Anglers and Hunters – David Gibson; Ontario Ministry of Natural Resources – Dr. John Casselman; Ontario Ministry of Tourism and Recreation – Tom Adamchick; Ontario Wilderness Houseboats Ltd. – Stew Gill; Steve Payne; Wayne Phillips; Promas, Inc. – Jim Speikers; Quebec Department of Recreation, Fish & Game – Michel Legault; Larry Ramsell; Bob Rife; Royal Ontario Museum – Dr. E. J. Crossman, Bernard Lebeau; George Sandell; Jake Satonica; Sentier, Chasse et Pêche – Albert Hudon; John Spinda; Steamboat Bait and Tackle – Sam Gilkerson; Thorne Brothers, Inc. – Paul Thorne; J. L. Trabue Company – Frank Harriman; University of Minnesota – Dr. James Underhill; Vados Bait and Tackle Co. – Dave Genz, Gordy & John Vados; West Virginia Department of Natural Resources – Bernie Dowler; Chuck Wilbert; Mark Windels; Wisconsin Department of Natural Resources – Dave Ives, Stan Johannes, Terry Margenau, John Peterson, Scott Stewart; Mike Woodside

Cooperating Manufacturers: Abu-Garcia, Inc.; Alumacraft Boat Company; Fred Arbogast Company, Inc.; Bagley Bait Company; Berkley, Inc.; Blue Fox Tackle Company; Bobbie Bait Company; Cannon/S & K Products, Inc.; Cobb's Famous Action Lures; Crane Custom Baits; D & K Distributors, Inc.; Daiwa Corporation; Dolphin Supplies, Inc.; Eddie Bait Company; Eppinger Mfg. Company; Feldman Eng. & Mfg. Co., Inc.; Fenwick; Fudally Tackle Company; GNB Inc./Stowaway Batteries; Dick Gries Tackle Company; H. T. Enterprises, Inc.; Herrick Enterprises/Wave Wackers; Jack's Jigs; Luhr Jensen & Sons, Inc.; Johnson Fishing, Inc./Minn Kota Trolling Motors; Bill Lewis Lures, Inc.; Lowrance Electronics, Inc.; Lund Boats; Mason Tackle Company; Mercury Marine-Mariner Outboards; Mouldy's Tackle Company; Nordic Crestliner Boat Company; Normark Corporation; Northland Fishing Tackle; Peterson Tackle Company; Plano Molding Company; Pointmatic Corporation; C. C. Roberts Bait Company; St. Croix Rod Company; Si-Tex Marine Electronics, Inc.; Stidham Enterprises; Stren Fishing Line; Suick Lure Mfg. Company; Wahl's Eagle Tail Lures; Windels Tackle Company; Yamaha Motor Corp., USA

Color Separations: Hong Kong Scanner Craft Co. Ltd.
Printing: R. R. Donnelley & Sons, Co. (0292)

Copyright © 1992 by Cy DeCosse Incorporated
5900 Green Oak Drive
Minnetonka, Minnesota 55343
1-800-328-3895
All rights reserved

Library of Congress
Cataloging-in-Publication Data

Sternberg, Dick.
Northern pike & muskie / by Dick Sternberg.
p. cm. – (The Hunting & fishing library)
Includes index.
ISBN 0-86573-037-7
1. Pike fishing. 2. Muskellunge fishing. I. Title. II. Title: Northern pike and muskie. III. Series.
SH691.P6S76 1992   91-34050
799.1'753 – dc20   CIP

Also available from the publisher:
The Art of Freshwater Fishing, Cleaning & Cooking Fish, Fishing With Live Bait, Largemouth Bass, Panfish, The Art of Hunting, Fishing With Artificial Lures, Walleye, Smallmouth Bass, Dressing & Cooking Wild Game, Freshwater Gamefish of North America, Trout, Secrets of the Fishing Pros, Fishing Rivers & Streams, Fishing Tips & Tricks, Fishing Natural Lakes, White-tailed Deer

Contents

Introduction

Northern pike and muskellunge are romanticized in more myths and tall tales than any other freshwater gamefish. Typical of these is the legend of the "Emperor's Pike." The fish, supposedly caught in a German lake in 1497, measured 19 feet long and weighed 550 pounds. An engraved copper ring around its body told of its release 267 years earlier by Emperor Frederick II. Examination of the preserved skeleton, however, revealed a hoax. The backbone was pieced together from the vertebrae of several different fish.

If you're looking for "fish stories," you won't find them in this book. What you will find is a wealth of straight information on pike and muskies, along with hundreds of spectacular color photos, that will help you catch them more consistently.

In the opening section, "Understanding Pike & Muskie," you'll learn the basic differences between the two species and how they differ from their hybrid, the tiger muskie. We'll also explain how to recognize different muskie color phases. Actual underwater photos show you how the fish use their senses, how they feed and how they spawn. A list of the most common pike-muskie myths (and facts refuting them) rounds off the section.

"Where to Find Pike & Muskies," acquaints you with their seasonal movement patterns. Satellite photographs give you an unusual and highly informative look at every type of lake or river you're likely to fish, while close-up photos identify the spots to work at different times of the year.

Catching these powerful fish requires some specialized gear. "Equipment" shows you exactly what you need, from rods and reels to boats, motors and electronics to oversized nets, tackle boxes and bait containers.

"Basic Techniques for Pike & Muskies" walks you through every important artificial-lure and natural-bait method. We'll show you the best baits and lures and how to present them, as well as dozens of little-known tips to make your presentations more effective.

"Techniques for Special Situations" helps you deal with problem fishing circumstances. You'll learn the best techniques for fishing in dense weeds and woody cover, for ultraclear and low-clarity water and for cold-front conditions.

This section also explains how to tackle situations not familiar to most pike-muskie anglers, such as night fishing and fishing in coldwater pockets. We cover the latest ice-fishing methods and offer some crucial advice on catching trophy pike and muskies.

Finally, "Prime Pike & Muskie Waters" reveals current hot spots throughout the United States and Canada. You'll probably discover some choice fishing holes not too far from home.

This book buries all the old myths and brings you into the new era of pike-muskie fishing. Despite the fact that many waters are overfished and good-sized pike and muskies are getting harder to come by, we're confident that you'll be catching more and bigger fish than ever after reading this book.

Understanding Northern Pike & Muskie

NORTHERN PIKE (*Esox lucius*) – Also known as northern, great northern pike, jack, jackfish, pickerel, brochet, luce, gator, snake. The sides vary from dark green to olive green to brown, with gold flecks and 7 to 9 rows of yellowish to whitish, bean-shaped spots. The underside is white or cream-colored. The dorsal and anal fins, which are set far back on the body, vary from greenish to reddish with irregular black marks, as does the tail. The entire cheek and top half of the gill cover are scaled (left inset). The duckbill-shaped jaws have long, sharp teeth; the roof of the mouth, pads of shorter, recurved teeth. The underside of the jaw usually has 10 sensory pores (inset).

MUSKELLUNGE (*Esox masquinongy*) – Also called muskie, lunge, maskinonge and innumerable other local names. Resembles the pike in most respects, but the background color of the sides is light, rather than dark, and the tips of the tail are more pointed. The sides vary from greenish to brownish to silvery, usually with dark markings, but the marks may be absent. The white or cream-colored belly often has brownish or grayish spots. The fins vary from greenish to brownish to bloodred and usually have dark markings. The cheek and gill cover have scales only on the top half (left inset). The number of pores on the underside of the jaw varies from 12 to 20, but the count is usually 15 to 18 (right inset).

Pike & Muskie Basics

"...he weighed upwards of 170 pounds, and is thought to be the largest [pike] ever seen. Some time ago, the clerk of the local parish was trolling...when his bait was seized by this furious creature, which by a sudden jerk pulled him in, and doubtless would have devoured him also, had he not by wonderful agility and dextrous swimming escaped the dreadful jaws of this voracious animal."

from Sir Isaac Walton's The Compleat Angler - 1815

A sea of misinformation surrounds the northern pike and muskellunge. Even today, we hear stories of huge pike or muskies attacking swimmers or charging outboard motors. Such tales make good copy in magazine articles, but only serve to perpetuate the "evil" image of these fish.

Of course, pike and muskies are the top predators in any body of water, and they'll eat larger prey than most other freshwater fish. But they're not the ruthless killers they're commonly portrayed to be.

To become a proficient pike or muskie angler, one must put aside the backlog of misinformation about these fish and learn more about their behavior and biological requirements.

Northern pike and muskellunge, along with pickerel, are sometimes referred to as Esocids; they belong to the pike family, whose technical name is Esocidae.

Pickerel, because of their smaller size, are much less popular with anglers. Chain pickerel seldom exceed 5 pounds; redfin pickerel, 1 pound. Although this book features pike and muskies, many of the techniques (on a smaller scale) will work equally well for pickerel.

Northerns hybridize with all other Esocid species. The best-known hybrid, the *tiger muskie*, is a pike-muskie cross. Tiger muskies, which get their name from their distinct vertical bars (p. 10), are rare in nature because pike spawn so much earlier than muskies. But fish hatcheries can easily produce hybrids, and the fish have been widely stocked in the United States. "Hybrid vigor" makes them grow faster than either parent, at least for the first several years of

North American Northern Pike Range

Muskellunge Range

life. Tigers do not reach the ultimate size of purebred muskies because their life span is shorter.

Although pike and muskies have a great deal in common, their differences far outweigh their similarities. Pike occur naturally at northern latitudes throughout the world. Muskies, however, are native only to North America, and their range does not extend as far north.

Muskies seldom reach the population density of pike. Although they deposit just as many eggs, the hatch rate is lower, and because pike hatch earlier, they prey heavily on young muskies (p. 15).

Technically, both species are classified as *coolwater fish*, meaning that they prefer lower temperatures than warmwater fish such as bass, but warmer than coldwater fish such as trout. In reality, however, their temperature preferences differ considerably.

Muskies prefer water in the 67- to 72-degree range; small pike, about the same. But large pike (30+ inches) could almost be classed as coldwater fish, favoring water temperatures from 50 to 55 degrees. Pike also spawn (p. 15) and feed (pp. 17-18) at lower temperatures than muskies. Another difference: pike bite throughout the year; muskies are seldom caught in winter.

Compared to pike, muskies are more selective as to what they eat. They're known for their habit of following a lure, then turning away at the last second. But muskies can afford to be choosy; pike can't. Since muskies aren't as numerous, they face less food competition from other members of their breed. Pike must eat whatever they can whenever they can or be outcompeted.

Due to their finicky nature, muskies are commonly billed as "the fish of 10,000 casts." Stories often describe how an angler fishes for years to catch a single muskie. Such tales discourage many anglers from trying for muskies. It's true that muskie fishing can be tough, but it's not nearly as difficult as many writers would lead you to believe. Some muskie specialists land over 100 each season.

Because pike aren't as selective, they're much easier to catch. In a creel survey conducted on a Wisconsin lake, anglers removed 50 percent of the pike crop in a single season. Another reason pike fishing is easier: the fish don't seem to learn from past mistakes. Many anglers have caught a pike with a distinctive marking, released it and then caught it again the same day. Rarely does this happen with muskies.

The relative ease of catching pike makes them extremely vulnerable to overfishing (p. 24). In most heavily fished waters, pike over 10 pounds are unusual. But in remote areas, they commonly exceed 25 pounds. Muskies are less affected by fishing pressure and frequently reach weights of 35 pounds or more, even in waters pounded by anglers.

Currently, the world-record pike is a 55-pound, 1-ouncer caught in Lake Grefeern, Germany, in 1986. The muskie record is 69 pounds, 15 ounces and was taken in the St. Lawrence River, New York, in 1957. The record hybrid weighed 51 pounds, 3 ounces and was caught in Lac Vieux Desert on the Wisconsin-Michigan border in 1919.

All Esocids are excellent food fish, with lean, white, flaky, mild-tasting meat. They're often belittled because of the Y-bones in the meat, but the bones can easily be removed (refer to *Cleaning & Cooking Fish* and *Fishing Tips & Tricks*, both from The Hunting & Fishing Library). Muskies, however, are too scarce to kill for the meat. Release them to fight another day.

Mutants and Hybrids

SILVER PIKE. A mutant form of northern pike, the silver pike occurs throughout the pike's native range. The sides vary from bright silver to metallic blue or green and have no markings except silver or gold flecks on the scales.

TIGER MUSKIE (pike-muskie hybrid). Sides with irregular, narrow bars, often broken into spots, on a light greenish to brownish background. The tips of the tail are rounder than a muskie's. Usually has 12 to 13 jaw pores.

The Muskie Triangle

Muskie literature, both popular and scientific, commonly refers to three distinct color phases – clear, spotted and barred. But anglers who catch lots of muskies know that many of the fish don't quite fit into any of these categories. The muskie triangle demonstrates just how variable muskie coloration can be. At the points of the triangle are each of the distinct color phases; along the sides, intergrades between two color phases; in the center, a combination of all three. The intergrades are considerably more common than the distinct color phases.

CLEAR. The sides and fins have no spots or blotches.

CLEAR/SPOTTED. The front of the body is mostly clear; spots become more prominent toward the tail.

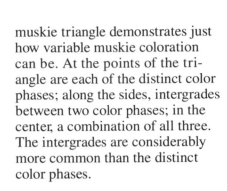

CLEAR/BARRED. The sides have dull bars that get progressively darker toward the tail.

SPOTTED/CLEAR/BARRED. The sides are almost clear at the front, but grade into a mixture of bars and spots that get darker toward the tail.

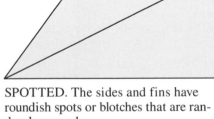

SPOTTED. The sides and fins have roundish spots or blotches that are randomly spaced.

SPOTTED/BARRED. The sides have a combination of spots and bars; spots are more prominent toward the rear.

BARRED. The sides have dark, vertical bars that are wider than those of a tiger muskie and not as broken.

Senses

Like most top-level predators, Esocids depend strongly on sight to find food. Their eyes are highly movable, enabling them to track fast-swimming prey and to see in practically any direction. The photo sequence on the opposite page demonstrates how a pike follows its prey with its eyes.

Evidence suggests that muskies are even more sight-oriented than pike. Muskies do not fare well in low-clarity waters, while pike thrive in murky lakes and rivers. Dutch researchers captured the same blind pike in the wild on three successive years; evidently the fish was feeding normally. In the early 1900s, German researchers blinded pike by cutting their optic nerves. Afterward, the pike could still catch live baitfish, presumably by using their other senses.

Muskies seem to have better night vision than pike, judging by the fact that they commonly take artificial lures after dark, while pike rarely do. Night feeders generally have a high ratio of rods (light receptors) to cones (color receptors) in their retina. There have been no studies to determine this ratio in muskies, but the ratio in pike is quite low, indicating a strong tendency toward daytime feeding.

Almost as important as vision is the lateral-line sense. An Esocid's lateral-line system includes lengthwise rows of pores along each side, as well as pores scattered over the body and head, including those on the underside of the jaw (p. 8). Slight vibrations in the water, such as those produced by swimming baitfish, activate tiny hairs inside the pores. The hairs, in turn, stimulate nerves inside and enable the fish to home in on its prey, even in murky water or under dim-light conditions. The lateral-line nerves in the head are especially important. The blinded pike mentioned above could not catch live baitfish after the nerves in their head were severed.

Reliance on their lateral-line sense explains why pike and muskies are drawn to lures that produce a lot of vibration, such as large-bladed spinnerbaits. Many anglers contend that you can often entice the fish to strike by changing the blades, and thus the pitch, of spinner-type lures.

The sense of smell is less important to pike and muskies than to most other freshwater fish. The lining of their nasal sacs has comparatively few *lamellar folds* and thus less surface area, so their sense of smell is less acute. One researcher studying the olfactory capability of pike concluded that they are "totally devoid of the capacity to respond to the smell of food."

But this conclusion is probably an overstatement. During coldwater periods, anglers frequently catch pike on dead baitfish, especially oily ones such as smelt, which have a strong odor. Muskies, on the other hand, rarely take dead baitfish.

The pores (arrow) scattered over the heads of pike and muskies are part of their lateral-line system

1. A 6-inch pike in an aquarium rests motionless on the bottom when not feeding.

2. When a small minnow is dropped into the water, the pike immediately rotates its eyes in the minnow's direction and assumes an alert posture. Keeping its eyes on the minnow, the pike begins to swim upward.

3. The pike stalks the minnow, moving slowly toward it while keeping its eyes riveted to the prey.

4. The pike strikes at incredible speed, taking the minnow and heading back to its resting position.

FEMALE PIKE are usually accompanied by one to three smaller males at spawning time. A male lines up alongside a female and slaps his tail under her body, releasing milt while she deposits a small batch of eggs. They repeat the act many times, often over 2 or 3 days, until all the eggs (up to 250,000 in a large female) are deposited.

Spawning

Northern pike and muskies are random spawners, not nest builders. They scatter their eggs in shallow water, most often over live or decaying aquatic plants or their roots.

Before spring breakup, pike in many lakes swim up tiny streams to spawn in adjacent marshes, which are ice-free. When the water temperature reaches 40 to 45° F, they deposit their eggs in water only 6 inches to 3 feet deep. In lakes without spawning marshes, pike spawn in weedy bays shortly after ice-out.

Muskies spawn 2 to 5 weeks later than pike, normally at water temperatures from 49 to 59° F. Seldom do muskies move into the spawning marshes used by pike. They often spawn in the same weedy bays of the main lake, but they drop their eggs in slightly deeper water.

In the Great Lakes and some other large lakes, muskies often spawn on shallow flats in large bays, far from the shoreline. They deposit their eggs in water as deep as 6 feet.

Males move onto the spawning grounds a few days earlier than females. Spawning lasts for 5 to 10 days. As the eggs and milt are released, males thrash their tails wildly, evidently to help scatter the eggs. The violent activity commonly results in deep gashes and split fins and may even kill the fish.

A few days after depositing their eggs, females leave the spawning area. Males usually stay around for several weeks, but do not protect the eggs. With no parents guarding them, the eggs are vulnerable to predators such as crayfish, predacious insects and small fish. The eggs that survive hatch in about two weeks. After their mouths develop, the fry begin feeding on plankton.

The hatch rate of the eggs is highly variable, but pike eggs hatch at a much higher rate than muskie eggs. Pike eggs sink slowly and are adhesive, so they cling to vegetation. Muskie eggs sink more rapidly and are not adhesive, so many of them settle into the mud and die from lack of oxygen.

In waters with both pike and muskies, pike fry get a head start because of the difference in spawning time. Consequently, they're larger and can easily prey on muskie fry. In one experiment, 25,000 pike fry and 25,000 muskie fry were stocked in a pond. A month later, 409 pike, but only 4 muskies, remained. When selecting waters to stock with muskies, fisheries managers look for lakes and rivers with relatively low pike populations. Otherwise, muskie fry wouldn't survive.

Anglers should understand how the spawning cycle affects fishing. Pike and muskies feed during the days before spawning and are catchable until spawning begins. They're seldom caught when spawning is in progress, but they start to bite again soon after it's completed. The whereabouts of large female muskies, however, is a mystery in the weeks after spawning. Some anglers believe that they go deep or suspend in open water, but nobody knows for sure.

Pike fry prey on the younger muskie fry

LARGE PREY is digested gradually by Esocids. This sequence shows a small northern pike ingesting a shiner about one-third its own length. The pike (1) grabs the prey crosswise, puncturing it with long, sharp teeth until it stops struggling. It then (2) turns the shiner and begins to swallow it head first. The shiner is much too large to be

Feeding Behavior & Growth

"I have always believed that a bounty should be paid for big muskies. Their appetites are voracious. Often they kill for the sheer fun of it, and the destruction they can do in an hour is appalling."

Harry Botsford – Field and Stream magazine - August 1956

Writings like this have contributed to the widespread misunderstanding of muskies and pike. Often called "water wolves," these toothy predators inspire wild visions in the minds of the uninformed. As a result, many anglers have the attitude that the fish shouldn't be stocked in their waters for fear of wiping out bass, walleyes and other "more desirable" gamefish. The following discussion summarizes the latest research into the feeding habits and growth of pike and muskies.

FEEDING HABITS. In reality, pike and muskies consume about the same amount of food in comparison to their weight as most other freshwater fish. What probably kindles so many fantasies is the way these fish feed. The young do not hesitate to attack other fish of nearly their own size, grabbing the prey by the head and swimming about with the tail sticking out of their mouth until they digest enough to swallow a little more. Occasionally, one of them chokes on the oversized food and dies with the prey lodged in its throat. Adult pike and muskies will eat fish from one-fourth to one-half of their own length, and up to 20 percent of their own weight.

Shortly after hatching, pike and muskie fry start to feed on plankton. As they approach an inch in length, they begin feeding on tiny insects. At about 2 inches, they switch to a diet consisting mainly of small fish, including their own kind.

Throughout the rest of their lives, fish continue to make up the bulk of their diet, but they will eat practically anything within the acceptable size range, including frogs, crayfish, mice, muskrats and ducklings. There have been reports of big pike and muskies

swallowed completely, but (3) the pike swallows as much as it can, letting the tail protrude from its mouth while the front end is being digested. (4) As digestion continues, only the tip of the shiner's tail is visible. Sometimes the tail still protrudes from the mouth 24 hours after the prey was struck.

attacking small dogs and even humans, although many such stories are greatly exaggerated.

Given a choice, both species would choose a soft-finned, cylindrical-bodied forage fish, such as a sucker, over a deep-bodied, spiny-rayed fish, such as a sunfish. The latter type would be harder to swallow and more likely to lodge in their throat. But in reality, pike and muskies eat plenty of sunfish, perch and other spiny-rayed fish, probably because they're commonly found in Esocid habitat.

Considered "sprint predators," pike and muskies usually lie in wait in some type of cover, intently ob-

The S-position prior to the strike

serving their prey. At the opportune moment, they cock their body into an "S," then dart forward, striking the prey at speeds approaching 30 miles per hour.

Once Esocids grab their prey, patches of sharp, recurved teeth on the roof of their mouth and their tongue prevent it from escaping while they gore it with their larger teeth, which have extremely sharp edges (p. 18).

Because pike and muskies feed mainly by sight, they're most active in daylight hours. But in clear lakes, or in waters with heavy fishing or boating activity, muskies do much of their feeding at night.

As experienced pike and muskie anglers know, the fish feed most heavily in overcast weather. Under sunny skies, they turn on just before sunset, although there may be a burst of feeding activity in early morning. Fishing is generally better with a light-to-moderate chop than a glassy surface. An approaching storm spurs a flurry of activity. Muskies turn off after a cold front, but pike continue to feed.

The peak feeding temperature for adult pike is about 65° F. They feed year around, but if the water

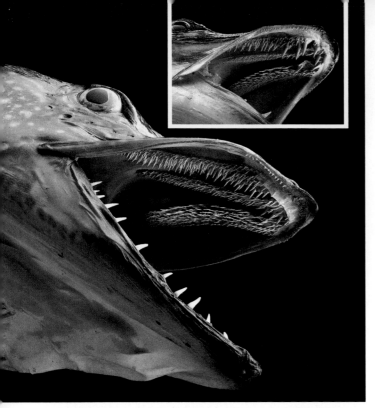

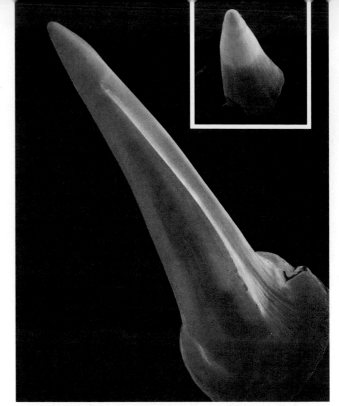

TEETH of Esocids are ideal for holding and killing prey. The *dentary* teeth, seen on the lower jaw of this mounted pike, pierce the prey while the tooth pads on the roof of the mouth prevent it from escaping. Large canine teeth on the roof of a muskie's mouth (inset) hold bigger prey.

RAZOR-SHARP EDGES on Esocid teeth are apparent in this electron microscope photograph. The teeth pierce and cut prey better than walleye teeth (inset), which are nearly round. This also explains why pike and muskies can easily bite off monofilament line, while walleyes can't.

temperature exceeds 75 in summer, the quantity of food they consume drops dramatically.

Poor summertime pike fishing is mainly a result of this feeding slowdown, not loss of teeth (p. 26) as many anglers believe. If pike can find cooler water, however, they will continue feeding.

Pike go on a feeding binge from late fall to early winter, presumably to nourish developing eggs and testes, but by midwinter, food consumption drops to about 10 percent of the maximum level.

Muskies feed very little until the water warms to 50° F in spring. Feeding peaks at about 70, and some feeding continues until the water reaches 80. The fish consume more food as the water cools in fall, but they seldom feed once the water temperature drops below 40.

GROWTH. How fast pike and muskies grow and the ultimate size they attain varies tremendously from one body of water to another. In many lakes, pike become so numerous that they dramatically reduce the crop of forage fish, resulting in severe stunting. Lakes with plenty of high-fat forage, such as ciscoes or smelt, produce considerably fewer pike, but the fish are big and deep-bodied.

Although anglers often accuse muskies of cleaning out all the forage in a lake, rarely do the fish become numerous enough to cause a food shortage. As a result,

stunting is a far less serious problem with muskies than with pike.

Water temperature also affects growth. Pike grow fastest at a water temperature of about 66° F; muskies, about 73.

The rapid growth of northerns in cool water explains why deep lakes usually produce bigger pike than do shallow ones. In summer, shallow lakes warm uniformly from top to bottom, so pike cannot find cool water. When forced to live at temperatures well above their comfort range, they grow slowly and their life span is much shorter than normal.

In warm water, pike seldom live more than 6 years; muskies, 12. But in cool water, both species may live 25 years or more. The Canadian-record muskie, a 65 pounder, was determined to be 30 years old.

Pike reach a maximum size about two-thirds that of muskies. The North American record pike weighed 46 pounds, 2 ounces; the record muskie, 69 pounds, 15 ounces. Pike from Europe and Asia approach the muskie's maximum size. The largest well-documented Eurasian pike weighed 67 pounds, 4 ounces.

On the average, Eurasian pike outweigh North American pike of the same length by about 13 percent. Pike genetics differ very little throughout their range, so it's uncertain why Eurasian pike are heavier-bodied.

Slow-growing vs. Fast-growing Pike

FAST-GROWING pike (top) have deep, wide bodies, often with relatively small heads. Slow-growing pike, commonly called "hammer handles" (bottom), have very skinny bodies and comparatively large heads.

Growth Rates of Muskies and Pike at Different Latitudes

	Length in Inches at Various Ages												
MUSKIES	Age 1	2	3	4	5	6	7	8	9	11	13	15	17
Maskinonge Lake, ON (50° N)	—	—	22.0	24.1	27.2	27.4	27.7	29.1	30.1	34.5	—	40.0	—
Lac Court Oreilles, WI (46° N)	8.6	15.3	20.5	24.8	27.2	29.8	31.6	33.0	36.4	—	—	—	—
Kawartha Lakes, ON (44° N)	6.9	17.5	23.7	28.1	31.2	34.3	36.6	38.6	40.4	43.5	46.0	48.2	—
Conneaut Lake, PA (42° N)	6.7	15.0	21.5	27.0	31.1	34.7	37.7	40.5	44.6	47.2	50.4	54.0	—
Piedmont Lake, OH (40° N)	15.5	22.3	29.9	33.7	36.3	38.2	40.9	43.0	47.3	—	—	—	—
Pomme de Terre Lake, MO (38° N)	12.2	22.1	29.1	35.2	36.7	39.7	42.2	45.5	—	—	—	—	—
NORTHERN PIKE													
Great Slave Lake, NWT (62° N)	4.2	6.3	8.6	11.1	13.2	15.5	17.5	19.6	21.3	24.7	28.6	33.5	36.2
Saskatchewan River Delta, SK (54° N)	4.2	8.9	14.7	19.7	22.0	23.1	24.8	27.3	31.5	—	—	—	—
Savanne Lake, ON (48° N)	9.6	13.8	16.6	19.3	21.7	24.4	27.3	30.8	33.5	36.5	—	—	—
Lake Vermilion, MN (47° N)	7.6	12.8	16.8	19.9	22.5	25.6	29.0	32.7	34.6	38.9	—	—	—
Lake Mendota, WI (43° N)	11.4	21.3	26.9	30.3	33.7	36.3	37.9	39.1	—	—	—	—	—

Pike & Muskie Habitat

The circumpolar distribution of northern pike reflects their ability to adapt to a wide variety of habitat. Their North American range extends from 40 to 70° N, well above the Arctic circle. They've been widely stocked throughout the Great Plains and Rocky Mountain States.

Pike exist in practically every type of water, from warm, shallow ponds, to deep, cold lakes, to muddy rivers. They even live in brackish areas of the Baltic

Sea. Their broad tolerance range for water temperature, water clarity and dissolved oxygen content makes them one of the most adaptable freshwater fish species.

Although pike, especially good-sized ones, prefer cool water, they can endure temperatures into the low 80s. But if they cannot find cool water in summer, they grow slowly and don't live long. Pike can tolerate very low clarity and oxygen levels and are among the last gamefish to die when a lake winterkills.

Muskies also inhabit a variety of lakes and rivers, but they're not nearly as versatile as pike. Found

only in North America, their native range extends from 36 to 51° N, barely reaching into Canada.

Like pike, muskies can survive in a wide range of water temperatures. But they're seldom found in waters with a maximum summer temperature below 68° F. They can tolerate water temperatures up to the mid 80s. Muskies prefer clear water and cannot adapt to water that stays turbid most of the time. They require considerably higher oxygen levels than pike.

Another important difference: muskies have a well-defined home range; pike don't. Several radio-tagging studies have shown that muskies seldom leave their home range, except to spawn, although they roam about within it. The larger the body of water, the larger the home range.

Both species prefer shallow, weedy water (less than 20 feet deep) during their early years of life. But as they grow larger, they spend more of their time in deep water. This tendency is stronger in pike than in muskies.

Pike and muskies will not tolerate fast current, so they're seldom found in rivers with a gradient (drop) of more than 10 feet per mile. If there are backwater areas where they can get out of the moving water, however, they'll live in rivers with higher gradients and faster current.

OLIGOTROPHIC LAKES (p. 34). Northern pike are native to nearly all "oli" lakes; muskies to only a few. Many of these lakes are north of the muskie's range (p. 9) and are too cold to support stocked muskies. Despite their deep, cold, infertile water and short growing season, oli lakes yield some of the continent's largest pike and muskies. But these lakes produce fewer pounds of fish per acre than most other pike-muskie waters, so even moderate fishing pressure can dramatically reduce the number of good-sized fish that are caught.

MESOTROPHIC LAKES (p. 32). These moderately fertile lakes produce more pike and muskies than any other type of water. Pike occur naturally in practically all "meso" lakes throughout the north country; muskies are native to only a few, but have been stocked in many others.

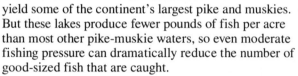

EUTROPHIC LAKES (p. 31). Pike are native to most of these fertile lakes in the North; muskies are commonly stocked. Most shallow eutrophic lakes have no coldwater refuge, so the pike are short-lived and seldom reach trophy size. Stocked muskies, however, occasionally grow to 50 pounds.

SHALLOW RESERVOIRS (p. 36). This class of man-made lakes includes flatland reservoirs, lowland reservoirs and *flowages*. Typically, these lakes are no deeper than 50 feet. The main basin is wide; the creek arms, short. Many have native pike populations, but muskies are usually stocked.

MID-DEPTH RESERVOIRS (p. 39). Known as hill-land, highland, cove and plateau reservoirs, these man-made lakes lie in hilly or mountainous terrain. They have a narrow main basin, long creek arms and maximum depths from 50 to 200 feet. Pike and muskies are usually stocked.

MID-SIZE RIVERS (p. 40). These rivers usually lack the diverse habitat provided by bigger rivers. Pike and muskies generally live in deep pools because there are few backwaters or side channels. In most cases, the fish are natural, not stocked.

BIG RIVERS (p. 42). Nearly all big, north-country rivers, particularly those with extensive backwater systems, have native pike populations. Muskies are also found naturally in some big rivers, but many of these waters are too muddy for muskies to survive.

This photo shows the results of the famous "muskie rampage" that occurred during two days of hot, muggy weather in 1955 on Minnesota's

Threats to Pike & Muskie Fishing

Throughout much of the northern pike's range, over-fishing has resulted in a dramatic decline in average size of the fish. Because pike are so aggressive, even moderate fishing pressure may cause problems. The results of overfishing are soon obvious. The big, deep-bodied pike disappear and are replaced with a much denser population of skinny, underfed pike that weigh less than 2 pounds.

Because of the catch-and-release ethic among muskie anglers and minimum-size restrictions, the decline in average size of muskies has not been as dramatic as that of pike. Many states have recently imposed higher minimum-size limits to further reduce the harvest of small- to medium-sized muskies. Although big muskies are harder to come by than they were a few decades ago, an impressive number of good-sized fish are caught each year.

To provide quality pike fishing in the future, conservation agencies in some states and provinces have established regulations to limit the harvest of big pike. And it's likely that many more agencies will follow suit in the near future.

Despite the trend toward more stringent pike regulations, a few states and provinces still allow darkhouse

Decoys attract pike, making them an easy target for spearers

Leech Lake. Some prefer to call it the "muskie massacre."

banks or agricultural lands in the watershed, or from pollution. Although muskies can tolerate turbid water for a short time, they disappear when it persists for a prolonged period. They cannot feed as well as they should, and sedimentation may smother their eggs.

Perhaps the most serious and difficult-to-solve problem facing pike and muskies is the destruction of spawning habitat. Often, developers fill in or damage prime spawning marshes to build homes or shopping centers. Spawning habitat also suffers when lake-

The fish won't spawn where the weeds have been removed

shore property owners remove nuisance weeds for easier boat access or sand their beaches to improve swimming conditions.

Roughfish can also destroy spawning habitat. Carp, for instance, move into weedy bays when the water warms in spring, roiling the shallows and rooting up vegetation that provides a base for the eggs and cover for the fry.

Yet another reason for loss of spawning habitat: a rapid increase in water fertility, usually the result of agricultural or municipal wastes draining into a lake or stream. When water fertility increases too much, the oxygen level at the bottom drops so low that the eggs cannot survive.

spearing in winter. This practice is a throwback to the days when pike were regarded as "snakes," fish not qualified for gamefish status. Studies have shown that spearers are more proficient at taking big pike than anglers. And there's no doubt that pike size has declined dramatically in almost all heavily speared lakes. Michigan and South Dakota also allow dark-house spearing of muskies on certain waters.

Several states permit underwater spearing of pike with SCUBA gear and in Vermont, you can shoot pike in spawning streams with handguns.

As discussed earlier, predation on young muskies by young pike is a widespread problem (p. 15). One common solution is to raise muskies to fingerling size, about 12 inches, so they're no longer vulnerable to predation by young pike. Another potential solution: stock a variety of muskie, such as the Leech Lake strain, that spawns in the middle of large bays, far from the shoreline vegetation used by spawning pike. This way, when the muskie eggs hatch, there are no pike lying in wait to eat the fry.

Increasing turbidity levels in many streams have resulted in serious declines in muskie populations. The problem usually results from erosion of stream-

Egg survival in this type of lake is very low

25

Pike- & Muskie-Fishing Myths

The impressive size and voracious feeding habits of these top predators spur the imagination of even the most rational anglers. The result is a multitude of misconceptions, some of which perpetuate the belief that pike and muskies are undesirable species.

Myth #1 – The muskies in my lake are eating all the other gamefish.

This belief often prevails around waters recently stocked with muskies. While there's no doubt that muskies eat some gamefish, they're rarely numerous enough to have a significant impact on other gamefish populations. A dense pike population poses a much greater threat.

Myth #2 – Pike are no good to eat.

True, they have a lot of "Y-bones," but the bones are easy to remove and the deboned meat is white, firm, flaky and excellent-tasting. In fact, many fish connoisseurs prefer pike to walleye. The eating quality of a muskie is similar to that of a pike, but thanks to catch-and-release fishermen, muskies are seldom taken for food.

Myth #3 – Pike and muskies lose their teeth in summer, get sore mouths and don't feed.

The fish shed teeth continuously as old ones break or work loose. The shedding is no greater in summer, and the fish don't get sore mouths. If fishing slows in summer, it's for one of the following reasons:

- Because of the abundance of natural food, the fish are less likely to take an angler's bait than in periods when food is scarce.

- Pike feeding may slow in summer as a result of high water temperatures (p. 18), but in most waters, muskies feed heavily all summer long.

- The fish have moved deeper than the majority of anglers are fishing.

Myth #4 – Pike always hang out in the weeds.

Small pike definitely spend most of their time in shallow, weedy areas. And big pike (more than 30 inches long) frequent shallow weeds in spring. But when the water warms in summer, the big ones usually move to deeper, cooler water.

Myth #5 – Pike and muskies don't bite at night.

It's true that pike do most of their feeding in daylight hours. Muskies are more prone to night feeding, especially in clear lakes. Tiger muskies have intermediate night-feeding tendencies.

Myth #6 – I've seen the same muskie in the same spot many times.

Although muskies have a smaller home range than pike, they move about more than most anglers believe. Just because you saw a muskie in a certain spot today is no guarantee it will be there tomorrow. The larger the body of water, the larger the muskies' home range and the more they tend to roam.

A certain piece of cover, such as a fallen tree, may hold a muskie most of the time, but it may not be the same fish. Even when a muskie is caught and removed, another similar-sized fish is likely to move in because the spot offers the right combination of food and cover for a fish of that size.

Myth #7 – Muskies don't bite in the spring.

Muskies prefer warmer water than pike, so it's true that they feed less actively in spring. They also spawn later than pike, so they may not be fully recuperated from the effects of spawning by the time the season opens. Or they may be in transition, moving from their spawning areas to their early summer locations. If you can find them, they'll bite, but you may have to use smaller-than-normal lures and slower retrieves.

Myth #8 – Muskies are loners.

Although magazine articles commonly make this contention, the fact is that muskies usually hang out in loose groups in certain key areas. The fish appear to be loners because they're difficult to catch and anglers seldom take more than one of them out of a given spot.

New York fisheries crew with a 65- to 70-pound muskie netted in Chautauqua Lake in the 1940s. A huge fish – but not a 100-pounder.

Myth #9 – Conservation departments have netted many 100-pound-plus muskies.

There has never been a documented 100-pound muskie taken anywhere. All reports of 100-pounders have proven to be hoaxes or simply exaggerations as word-of-mouth reports spread from angler to angler. Even when conservation workers do net large fish, they rarely have accurate scales.

Myth #10 – The muskies you see suspended just beneath the surface are sick.

For some unknown reason, muskies seem to enjoy "sunning" themselves. On calm, sunny days, they'll often lie motionless with their backs almost out of the water. But the fish are perfectly healthy and are sometimes catchable, if you can approach without spooking them.

Where to Find Pike & Muskies

"Jingle Bells," a monster pike that once terrorized a northern Wisconsin lake, reputedly broke so many lines that all the spoons hanging from his jaws jingled when he jumped.

The tendency of pike and muskie anglers to attach such colorful names to their quarry results from the mistaken belief that the fish are homebodies, seldom wandering far from a certain weedbed or log.

But recent radio-tagging studies have proven what many expert anglers already knew: the fish, particularly northern pike, cover a lot more territory than most fishermen think.

Most studies have shown that pike do not have a well-defined home range. They move about in response to food supply and water temperature, variables that tend to change with the seasons. Although muskies are less mobile, they may roam an area of more than 10,000 acres in a large lake.

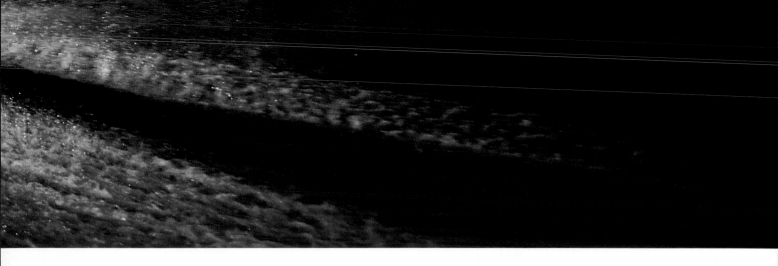

Not to say that pike and muskies will never be found in the same place from one week to the next. A dominant fish may have a spot it routinely frequents.

But more likely, the big fish you've seen next to the same log several times is, in fact, several different fish relating to a spot that fulfills all the needs of a fish of that size.

Concentrating on a particular spot or a specific area may pay dividends for a while, but for consistent pike- or muskie-fishing success from one season to the next, you must become familiar with their seasonal movement patterns in the type of water you fish.

In waters that contain both pike and muskies, the two often use the same habitats. But because pike prefer cooler water, they may not occupy the habitat at the same time as muskies.

For instance, pike move into shallow spawning bays several weeks earlier than muskies. The first hot days of summer usually drive big pike out of the bays, but muskies hang around a few weeks longer and some may not leave until late fall.

The following pages will show you where to find pike and muskies during each season in various types of natural lakes, reservoirs and rivers.

LILY-PAD BEDS provide overhead cover and keep the water a few degrees cooler in summer. Look for pike and muskies along deep, outside edges.

SHALLOW, WEEDY BAYS of the main lake are the primary pike-muskie spawning grounds. Pike will also spawn in adjoining marshes.

ROCK BARS or sand bars adjacent to deep water are good pike-muskie producers in fall. Shallow bars often have bulrushes on top.

WEEDY BARS, points and flats are good pike-muskie spots in summer. Look for slick water or protruding weed tips.

Eutrophic Lakes

DEEP BULRUSH FIELDS along shoreline flats draw pike and muskies from late summer through fall, when cabbage and other submerged weeds begin to die off.

HARD-BOTTOMED POINTS, reefs and breaklines near spawning bays attract post-spawn pike and muskies. Structure with new emergent weed growth is best.

SPRINGS draw pike in summer because there is no other coldwater refuge. The deep water usually lacks oxygen.

These shallow lakes warm earlier than other natural lakes, so they provide better early-season pike and muskie action. Most eutrophic lakes, because of their high fertility, do not have sufficient oxygen in the depths much of the year, so the fish are confined to shallow water. Even when there is enough oxygen, the fish still don't go deep. The light level below 10 feet is usually too low for weeds to grow and for the fish to see well.

Esocids in eutrophic lakes can choose from a smorgasbord of baitfish, ranging from sunfish to small bass to bullheads and other roughfish. Some of these lakes produce up to 300 pounds of forage per acre of water per year.

But this much food may create problems for anglers. Feeding periods tend to be short, especially in summer, when food is most abundant. Summertime fishing is especially tough in lakes with heavy algae blooms. The reduced clarity makes it difficult for the fish to see your bait.

Your best chances are in spring, before the young baitfish hatch, and in fall, after the year's crop has been whittled down and the water clears.

Because eutrophic lakes are the first to cool in fall, they're the first to offer good fall fishing. But they're also the first to get too cold for good muskie action.

Pike feed heavily until a few weeks after the ice forms, usually in shallow, weedy bays. The action slows considerably in midwinter, when they spread out over bars, flats, points and deep basins in the main lake.

Mesotrophic Lakes

Pike and muskie location in meso lakes depends mainly on water depth and type of forage. Yellow perch are the major food source in shallower meso lakes; ciscoes, in deeper ones.

In perch lakes, pike and muskies spend most of their time in close proximity to weedbeds and drop-offs, the areas where perch are normally found. In many of these lakes, the oxygen content below the thermocline falls too low for pike and muskies by late summer, confining the fish to the shallows. The oxygen level rebounds following the fall turnover, allowing the fish to go deeper.

Pike and muskies in cisco lakes spend a good deal of their time suspended in or over deep water once they complete spawning. The oxygen level in the depths is adequate through the summer, so it does not affect their movements.

In late fall, pike and muskies follow the ciscoes onto their spawning grounds. Ciscoes begin to congregate in the shallows when the water drops to 45 degrees; spawning begins at about 40 degrees and peaks at 38. The "cisco" pattern produces some of the year's best fishing, particularly for trophy-sized fish.

As a rule, cisco lakes produce larger pike and muskies than perch lakes, although both types can produce trophy fish. The food itself may not be as much a determinant of size as the structure of the lake. Because cisco lakes are deeper, they offer a permanent coldwater refuge for pike, meaning a longer life span. Also, because pike and muskies spend so much time cruising open water for suspended forage, they're less vulnerable to angling.

WEEDY POINTS attract pike and muskies all summer. Points with an extended lip are better than those that drop rapidly from shore.

BULRUSH BANKS are excellent pike and muskie producers in late summer and fall. The best banks have a deep, irregular margin.

CONNECTING MARSHES are prime spawning areas for pike. The young, along with some small males, stay in the marshes until midsummer.

WEEDY SADDLES between two islands or an island and shore are reliable pike-muskie spots during the summer.

WEEDY BAYS, especially those fed by a creek, make good spawning areas for muskies and, in lakes without connecting marshes, pike. Smaller fish stay in the bays until fall.

SHALLOW REEFS and points that have rock-gravel bottoms and are near deep water make good cisco spawning areas and top late-fall pike-muskie spots.

GRAVEL BARS, points and shoreline breaks just outside the spawning bays hold pike and muskies after they finish spawning.

CABBAGE HUMPS that top off at 8 to 15 feet hold pike and muskies all summer. Rocky humps are a better choice in fall.

Oligotrophic Lakes

Latitude has a major effect on pike-muskie location in oligotrophic lakes. In the Far North, for instance, these lakes are so cold that pike stay in the bays all year. Even in midsummer, the bays seldom exceed 65° F, still within the comfort range of pike and of ciscoes, their main forage. There are no muskies in lakes this cold.

Pike move about much more in oli lakes farther south. There, the bays get too warm for big pike in summer, forcing them into the main lake. Some muskies, however, stay in the bays all year.

In the latter type of lake, the fish have a wider choice of food, including perch, suckers and minnows in the shallow, weedy parts of a lake; ciscoes, burbot and sometimes smelt in the deeper parts.

It's not unusual to find some pike and muskies suspended over open water in pursuit of ciscoes,

STREAM MOUTHS draw pike and muskies through the open-water season. The fish move in to feed on baitfish drawn by the current.

ISLAND CLUSTERS that form a large, continuous reef are excellent summertime locations, especially if the reef has patches of submerged weeds.

NARROWS between an island and shore or two islands usually have a wind-induced current that draws baitfish. Pike and muskies follow in summer and fall.

GRAVEL POINTS and shorelines that drop off rapidly make good cisco spawning areas. Pike and muskies move in when the water reaches the mid-40s.

while other fish are feeding on perch in shallow weedbeds.

Although pike and muskies grow slowly in most of these lakes, they live longer than in other waters, sometimes as long as 30 years. This explains why they grow so large in lightly fished oli lakes.

In the Far North, oli lakes remain icebound until late spring, but as soon as the ice goes out, pike action heats up. Fishing slows a little in midsummer, but picks up again in late summer. In oli lakes farther south, anglers enjoy a burst of pike and muskie action in mid- to late spring. Fishing is poor in mid-summer, begins to improve by late summer and peaks in mid- to late fall.

Ice fishing for pike can be good on these lakes, with most of the action confined to the shallow bays.

Springs and coldwater feeders seldom attract pike in oli lakes. Because of the abundance of cold, well-oxygenated water, the fish simply go deeper to avoid warmwater stress.

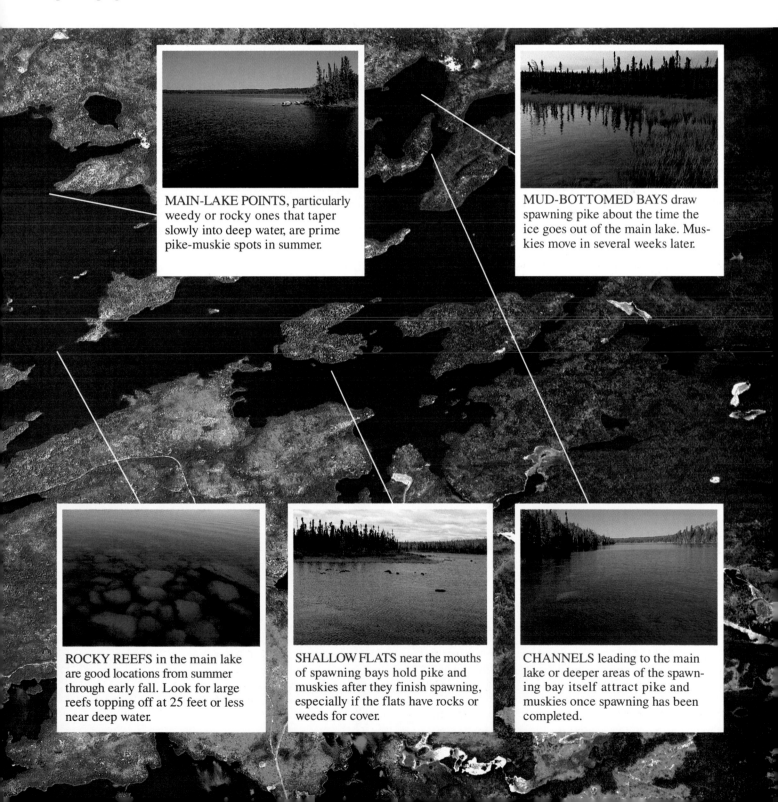

MAIN-LAKE POINTS, particularly weedy or rocky ones that taper slowly into deep water, are prime pike-muskie spots in summer.

MUD-BOTTOMED BAYS draw spawning pike about the time the ice goes out of the main lake. Muskies move in several weeks later.

ROCKY REEFS in the main lake are good locations from summer through early fall. Look for large reefs topping off at 25 feet or less near deep water.

SHALLOW FLATS near the mouths of spawning bays hold pike and muskies after they finish spawning, especially if the flats have rocks or weeds for cover.

CHANNELS leading to the main lake or deeper areas of the spawning bay itself attract pike and muskies once spawning has been completed.

Shallow Reservoirs

WOODEN "CRIBS" and other man-made fish attractors draw pike and muskies all year, especially in reservoirs with little natural cover.

Some of these reservoirs have highly fertile water, much like eutrophic lakes. Others are somewhat deeper and not as fertile, so they more closely resemble meso lakes.

In the former type of reservoir, the depths lose their oxygen during the summer, confining the fish to water less than 20 feet deep. Occasionally, these waters suffer winterkills. In the latter type, or in any reservoir fed by a good-sized stream, oxygen levels are adequate throughout the year, so the fish can go wherever they want.

These lakes are found where the terrain is quite flat. The dams are comparatively low, so the water has not risen enough to cover much of the timber. In young reservoirs, large areas of standing trees remain; in old reservoirs, only stumps and fallen treetops.

As reservoirs age, the old river channel gradually silts in to the point where it's barely noticeable. But even if the channel is subtle, it offers deeper water and often the most pronounced structure in the lake, so it still draws plenty of fish.

Although most of these lakes have plenty of naturally produced pike, the fish won't grow large unless there is enough oxygen in the depths or some other type of coldwater refuge in summer. Pike populations are usually too high to allow successful muskie reproduction (p. 15), but stocked muskies thrive because small panfish, minnows and other baitfish are so plentiful. In fact, the Chippewa Flowage, a shallow Wisconsin reservoir, produced a muskie weighing 69 pounds, 11 ounces, only 4 ounces shy of the current world record.

Shallow reservoirs warm rapidly in spring, so they offer good early-season fishing. But the action slows considerably in midsummer, when algae blooms cloud the water and massive schools of baitfish roam the shallows. Fishing perks up in early fall, when the algae dies back and predation thins out the baitfish.

FLATS and humps adjacent to the old river channel hold pike and muskies in summer and fall. Flats with stumps, standing timber or weeds are best.

DEEP POINTS and humps that break sharply into deep water are good pike-muskie locations in fall, once the submerged weeds die off.

SHALLOW POINTS that have stumps or weeds and are near the old river channel, are prime pike-muskie spots in summer and fall.

MARSHES and shallow, weedy bays connected to the river channel above the reservoir draw spawning pike and muskies.

SHALLOW CREEK ARMS make good spawning areas for pike and muskies. Pike return to deeper parts of creek arms in late fall and stay until midwinter.

COLDWATER FEEDERS flowing into back bays and creek arms attract pike from midsummer into early fall.

POINTS that extend into the creek channel and flats alongside the channel hold pike and muskies after they complete spawning.

TIMBERED HUMPS in the main lake, especially those near the old river channel, draw pike and muskies after cooling water scatters the baitfish in fall.

SECONDARY CREEK ARMS warm earlier than the main creek arms, so they're the first to attract spawning pike and muskies in spring.

MAIN-LAKE POINTS, especially those with extended lips, hold pike and muskies from summer through fall.

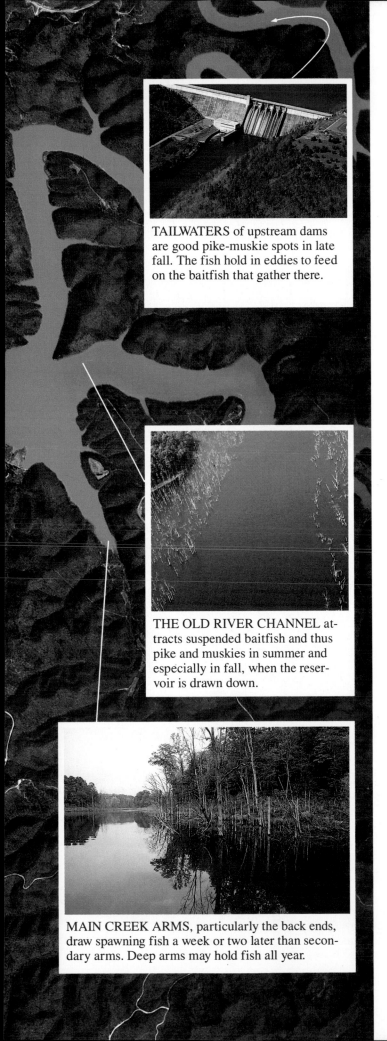

TAILWATERS of upstream dams are good pike-muskie spots in late fall. The fish hold in eddies to feed on the baitfish that gather there.

THE OLD RIVER CHANNEL attracts suspended baitfish and thus pike and muskies in summer and especially in fall, when the reservoir is drawn down.

MAIN CREEK ARMS, particularly the back ends, draw spawning fish a week or two later than secondary arms. Deep arms may hold fish all year.

Mid-Depth Reservoirs

Some mid-depth reservoirs are merely natural lakes with low-head dams that have raised the water several feet above the original level. But others have high dams and are used for flood control, so the water is drawn down as much as 50 feet in late fall to make room for spring runoff.

With this much fluctuation, rooted aquatic plants cannot grow. The only natural cover in these lakes is flooded timber, stumps, brush or rocks, but there's usually man-made cover such as old roadbeds, bridge pilings, house foundations and various types of fish attractors.

The dramatic fluctuations cause the fish to move much more than they would in lakes with stable water levels. Summertime hangouts may become dry land by late fall, so the fish have no choice but to head for any remaining deep water.

Pike are native to many mid-depth reservoirs in the Midwest; muskies to a few in the East and South. But the majority of these waters have been and continue to be stocked. The water fluctuations make for inconsistent spawning success.

Most mid-depth reservoirs have clear, moderately fertile water that supports large crops of suspended baitfish such as shad, smelt or shiners. Pike and muskies spend much of their time cruising open water in search of food. These feeding movements, combined with movements caused by water-level shifts, make it hard for anglers to keep track of the fish and put together a consistent pattern.

Because food is plentiful and fishing tough, the fish grow to impressive size in these waters. The Missouri River reservoirs in North and South Dakota, for instance, are known for catches of pike in the 20- to 30-pound class, and the North American record pike weighing 46 pounds, 2 ounces was caught in Sacandaga Reservoir in New York. Muskies over 40 pounds have been caught in dozens of mid-depth reservoirs in the South and East.

One good time to fish these waters is in spring, when fish move into the back ends of creek arms to spawn. Another is in fall, when drawdowns concentrate the fish on flats, humps and points in or near the old river channel and deep creek channels, and cooling water keeps them on the shallowest part of the structure.

Mid-Size Rivers

Pike and muskies thrive in many rivers where you could easily skip a rock from one bank to the other. The middle and lower reaches, where the river is wider and slower, usually hold more and bigger fish than the upper reaches. Most mid-size rivers lack extensive backwater systems, although there may be some shallow sloughs connected to the main channel.

One requirement, particularly for muskies, is relatively clear water. Rivers that carry a permanent silt load may support some pike, but will seldom hold muskies. Even rivers that lack permanent Esocid habitat sometimes produce pike. Anglers intercept them as they migrate between other lakes in the watershed.

Forage fish, usually suckers, redhorse and minnows, are plentiful in most mid-size rivers. Small gamefish, such as walleyes and smallmouth bass, often add to the food supply.

TAILWATERS of dams draw large concentrations of baitfish. Pike and muskies feed in eddies alongside the fast water most of the year.

POOLS at least 6 feet deep with light current may hold pike and muskies all year. The best pools have boulders or fallen trees.

IMPOUNDMENTS above low-head dams often have the deepest water in the river. They draw fish during low-water periods and are important wintering areas.

EDDIES below boulders, points, sharp bends or islands make good feeding stations. The fish can easily grab a meal, then return to the slack water.

Although most mid-size rivers produce comparatively small muskies, some are capable of growing fish in the 30- to 40-pound range. The biggest fish generally come from the largest pools. Pike in these waters are even less likely to reach trophy size because they're more vulnerable to anglers.

Pike fishing in connecting sloughs heats up in early spring as the fish move in to spawn. But if there are no sloughs, the action is slow until late spring or early summer, when the receding water confines pike and muskies to deep pools. The pools continue to produce until late fall, but if the water gets too low, they stagnate. Should this happen, the fish seek out areas with faster current, where the oxygen level is higher.

In deeper rivers, pike and muskies overwinter in the same pools where they spent the summer. In shallow rivers, however, they move out of their home pools in late fall and into impoundments above low-head dams (opposite page), where they stay until spring.

CURRENT BREAKS, where slow and fast water meet, hold pike and muskies when the water drops very low and the pools stagnate.

OXBOW LAKES, old channels cut off from the river, hold pike and muskies all year, if they're deep enough so they don't freeze out.

SPRINGS in old channels attract pike in summer and early fall, especially when the river is low and the water temperature rises into the 80s.

SLOUGHS adjacent to the river are good pike-muskie spawning areas, assuming springtime water levels are high enough to flood them.

TROUT STREAMS or any cold-water feeders entering backwaters, boat harbors or bays are prime hot-weather spots for big pike and, occasionally, muskies.

DEEP CUTS leading from the backwaters to the main channel hold pike and muskies in summer and fall.

LARGE EDDIES, such as those that form below islands, sharp bends, points, logjams, or gravel bars, attract pike and muskies in summer and fall.

BACKWATER LAKES serve as pike-muskie spawning areas in spring. Some fish remain in deeper backwater lakes all year.

Big Rivers

Big rivers offer premier fishing for trophy pike and muskies. In fact, the current world-record muskie, a 69 pound, 15 ouncer, was taken in the St. Lawrence River in New York. The St. Lawrence has produced 11 other muskies topping the 60-pound mark.

Rivers of this type generally have a greater diversity of habitat than mid-size rivers (p. 40). The main channel has holes at least 30 feet deep and the back-water system is usually much more extensive, consisting of shallow sloughs, deeper lakes and a maze of side channels. All of these connecting waters rise and fall in concert with the river.

Big rivers are fed by many small to mid-size rivers, some of which may be good pike-muskie producers. Low water may temporarily drive fish out of the tributaries and into the main river, and high water in the main river sometimes pushes fish into tributaries with slower current.

FLOODED SLOUGHS connected to the river are important spawning areas for pike. The fish will swim far up tiny feeders to reach these sloughs.

WEEDBEDS in side channels or the main channel attract pike and muskies from the time the weeds emerge in spring until they die in fall.

TAILWATERS below dams hold some pike and muskies all year, but they're best in spring, when the higher flow draws fish upstream.

Water clarity has a major impact on big-river pike and muskie location. In clear rivers, the fish do not hesitate to use water as much as 40 feet deep; in murky ones, they seldom go deeper than 15 feet. Often, siltation in the lower reaches of a river keeps the water too murky for muskies.

One reason big rivers produce so many trophy-class fish is the abundance and diversity of food, including many riverine baitfish seldom found in lakes. Another reason: changing water levels spell tough fishing much of the time. When the water rises or falls, even

a few inches, the fish move. And unless you're intimately familiar with their movement patterns, you can burn up a lot of time looking for them.

On rivers with a year-round fishing season, anglers enjoy a spurt of fast action when pike move into flooded backwaters to spawn. Sometimes, the backwaters produce muskies as well. After spawning is completed, however, the fish scatter and are difficult to find until the water drops back to its normal summertime level. Good fishing continues through the summer and well into fall.

Equipment

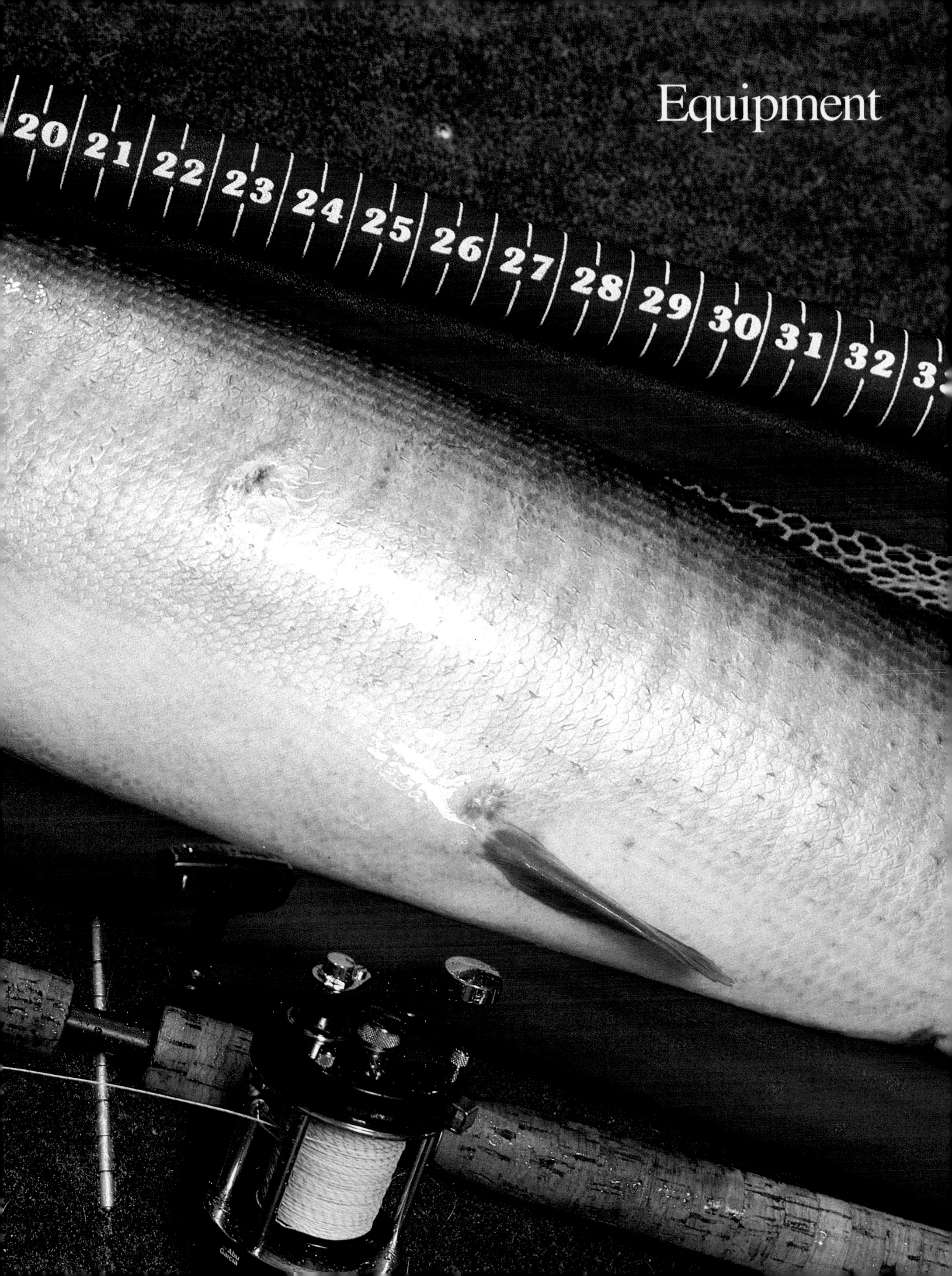

Rods, Reels, Lines & Leaders

A good pike-muskie outfit must be tough, yet light enough so it doesn't wear you out. Whether you prefer spinning or baitcasting gear, the trend is toward longer rods. Because of the improved tensile strength of rod-making materials, rods can be made longer without adding much weight. Although long rods are not the answer for all types of pike and muskie fishing, they offer the following advantages:

· Better casting accuracy and more distance.

· Better control on the retrieve. You can easily change direction to trigger strikes and steer your bait through weeds or other obstructions.

· Deeper figure eights (p. 60). With a short rod, you'd have to lean over the boat to get the lure deep enough, possibly spooking the fish. A long rod also gives you larger, smoother figure eights, making it easier for the fish to catch the lure.

· More hook-setting power. A long rod picks up slack line faster and gives you extra leverage.

· Better control of hooked fish. A longer rod helps you lead the fish and makes a better shock absorber.

Whatever rod you select, the tip should be made of silicone carbide

Bucktail rod

or carboloy; a stainless-steel tip will soon develop grooves and fray your line.

Baitcasting gear is generally more durable than spinning gear and is a requirement for Dacron line; it's also a better choice for heavy mono. When selecting a baitcasting reel, consider line capacity, smoothness of the drag, gear ratio and gear material.

For heavy line, use a large-capacity reel, preferably one with a wide spool. With a narrow one, the line level falls too low on a long cast, reducing distance and slowing your retrieve speed. Choose a reel with a high gear ratio (at least 4.5:1) when using lures that require a fast retrieve. For durability, the gears should be made of brass, not aluminum.

A smooth drag is essential because pike and muskies have the habit of making fast, powerful runs at boatside. If your drag sticks, the line may break or the hook could straighten or pull out.

Listed below are rod, reel, line and leader recommendations for different types of pike and muskie fishing. These outfits will easily cast large lures and pull big fish out of dense cover. If you prefer light lures and won't be fishing around obstructions, you can get by with ordinary bass-fishing gear and 10- to 15-pound mono.

FISHING WITH BUCKTAILS, SPINNERBAITS, SPOONS AND TOPWATERS. A 6½- to 7½-foot medium-heavy, fast-action baitcasting rod with a high-speed reel is ideal for these lures. Besides giving you extra casting distance and helping you guide the lures through slots in surface vegetation, a long rod makes it easier to bulge bucktails and spinnerbaits on the surface (p. 67).

Dacron line, 30- to 50-pound test, is the best choice for fishing these and most other shallow-running lures. It casts well, is more abrasion-resistant than mono, and has much less stretch, so you get stronger hook sets. Don't substitute braided nylon for Dacron. It stretches more and retains too much water.

Use a heavy, stainless-steel-wire leader with bucktails and spinnerbaits; a 20- to 30-pound braided-wire leader with topwaters and spoons. A heavy leader could sink the nose of a topwater and impair the action of a spoon. Some of these lures, especially spoons and bucktails, tend to spin on the retrieve, so your leader should have ball-bearing swivels.

FISHING WITH CRANKBAITS AND VIBRATING PLUGS. A 7- to 7½-foot, medium-heavy-power flippin' stick coupled with a high-speed, bass-sized baitcasting reel works well for this type of fishing. With the long, stiff rod and 15- to 20-pound low-stretch mono, you can snap off most vegetation that fouls your plug. Use a thin, flexible, braided-wire leader that won't restrict the lure's action and will cut through the weeds.

Crankbait rod

Standard trolling rod

Downrigger rod

MINNOW-PLUG FISHING. Most minnow plugs are easy to cast with crankbait gear. But spinning gear is better for light, wind-resistant models. Use a 6½- to 7½-foot, medium-heavy rod and a wide-spool, smooth-drag reel spooled with 10- to 15-pound mono. Attach these plugs to a thin, braided-wire leader with a light clip, not a heavy snap-swivel.

FISHING WITH TROLLING PLUGS. A stiff, 6-foot baitcasting rod and a wide-spool reel spooled with 20-pound mono make a good all-around trolling outfit. But some trollers, especially downrigger fishermen, prefer a fiberglass rod about 8 feet long; the extra flex allows use of lighter line.

Color-coded mono is ideal for trolling because it gives you precise depth control. For trolling in very deep water, use 30-pound single-strand-wire line and a stiff rod with a roller guide on the tip. Dacron line is too thick and buoyant for deep trolling.

Attach a 20- to 30-pound braided-wire leader for maximum plug action.

JERKBAIT FISHING. When a good-sized Esocid clamps down on one of these big, wooden lures, you'll need a stiff rod to dislodge it and move it far enough to sink the hooks. But don't use a "pool cue"; the rod should flex

Jerkbait rod

How to Make Wire Leaders

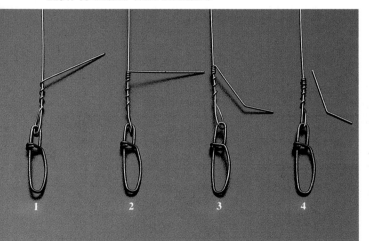

HAYWIRE TWIST (for single-strand wire). Make about (1) three loose twists followed by (2) five tight wraps. (3) Bend the free end into the shape of a handle, then (4) crank the handle several times to break off excess wire.

TWIST MELT (for nylon-coated wire). Twist the wire about five times (left). Then pass a lighter under the twists until the nylon melts together (right). Be sure to heat the nylon gradually or it will catch on fire. Trim the tag end.

enough so the hooks won't pull out when a big fish starts thrashing.

When retrieving jerkbaits, you bring the rod to a near-vertical position with each downward sweep (p. 82). With a rod that's too long, the tip would continually splash water. Select a rod that doesn't quite reach the water when held vertically from the position in which you normally stand in the boat. In most cases, that means a baitcasting rod no more than 6½ feet long.

Strong, low-stretch line is especially important in jerkbait fishing. Use 36- to 50-pound Dacron line and a stiff-wire leader.

JIG FISHING. Spinning tackle is the best choice for jigs up to ½ ounce. Select a 6-foot, medium-heavy, fast-tip rod with a long butt. Match it with a large-

Jigging rod

capacity, front-drag spinning reel spooled with 10- to 15-pound mono. Flippin' sticks, such as those used for crankbaits, work better for heavier jigs.

Use a foot-long, 20-pound, single-strand or braided-wire leader when jig fishing. A longer leader is unnecessary; rarely are the fish deeply hooked.

FLY-FISHING. To cast large flies and handle these hard-fighting fish, you'll need an 8- to 10-weight graphite rod from 8½ to 9 feet long and a weight-forward line such as a bass-bug taper. Use a sink-tip or full-sinking line with streamers or other sinking flies; a floating line with divers and other bugs. A single-action reel with interchangeable spools helps you switch lines quickly.

Use a 4- to 6-foot length of 30- to 40-pound-mono leader with a floating line; a 2- to 3-foot length with a sink-tip or sinking line. Add a foot of 15- to 40-pound nylon-coated braided wire to the end of your leader using an Albright knot (p. 87).

NATURAL-BAIT FISHING. Most natural-bait fishing can be done with the same outfit used for bucktail fishing. A long rod makes it easy to lob-cast the bait so you won't snap it off or injure it. And it gives you a strong hook set, even when using a slip-bobber in deep water. With a short rod, it's hard to take up all the slack when you set the hook. However, when retrieving live baitfish jerkbait-style (p. 95), a bucktail rod is too long. Use a jerkbait rod no longer than 6½ feet.

When you're still-fishing and a fish takes your bait, it should feel little resistance. A baitcasting reel with a clicker signals a bite, yet the fish can easily take line.

Most natural-bait fishing is done with 15- to 20-pound mono. Dacron line is not a good choice for still-fishing because it sinks too quickly, making it difficult to reel up slack when a fish bites. Always use a 20- to 30-pound braided-wire leader at least 2 feet long. Any shorter, and a big fish may cut the line if it swallows the bait. A heavier leader will restrict the bait's movement.

CRIMP (for braided wire). (1) Thread a metal sleeve onto the wire; pass the wire through the eye of a snap or swivel, then through the sleeve again. (2) Pass the wire through the sleeve once more. (3) Tighten, crimp and trim.

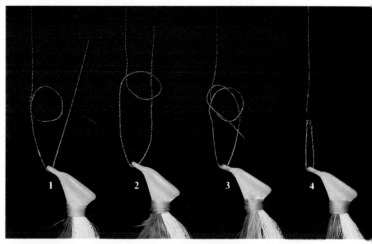

BOWLINE (for braided wire). (1) Thread free end through eye of lure or swivel; form loop in standing end. (2) Push free end through loop. (3) Wrap free end around standing end and through loop again. (4) Pull free end to tighten.

DEEP-V hulls work best for fishing pike or muskies on big water. A hull with a V shape all the way to the rear (inset) rides much smoother than a semi-V hull, which is V-shaped in front, but flat in the rear.

Boats, Motors & Accessories

You don't need an expensive boat and motor with the latest gadgetry to catch pike and muskies. But your rig must be suited to the type of water you fish and your style of fishing.

BOATS. Most fishing-boat manufacturers have at least one "pike" or "muskie" boat in their line. These boats usually have the following features:

· a 16- to 18-foot deep-V hull

· a large, open floor that can accommodate big tackle boxes, big nets and other bulky gear used in pike and muskie fishing

· an elevated casting platform in the bow and sometimes in the stern

· designed for a tiller-handle outboard

· a front deck large enough for a bow-mount trolling motor

But not all pike and muskie anglers agree on the ideal boat. Many, for instance, prefer console steering, especially if they have to run long distances. River and small-lake fishermen often use bass boats or jon boats, which are better suited to shallow water.

MOTORS. Your choice of motor depends not only on the weight and hull design of your boat, but also on your style of fishing. A 20-hp motor can easily push a stripped-down, 16-foot aluminum semi-V. But a 16-foot fiberglass tri-hull or a fully rigged 16-foot aluminum deep-V requires at least 50hp.

If you do a lot of backtrolling, you'll need a motor that runs slowly and smoothly in reverse. You probably won't have a problem with motors of 25hp or less, but many larger motors troll too fast. The gear ratio in reverse is too high, and unless they have more than 2 cylinders, they may run rough. The best way to find out how a motor trolls is to ask a fisherman who has one.

ACCESSORIES. A transom-mount electric motor works well for backtrolling in calm water, where even a slow-trolling outboard would move you too fast. For casting, a bow-mount electric is practically a must. Be sure the shaft is long enough so the prop stays beneath the surface in rough water. A foot control leaves your hands free for fishing, but a hand control is less cumbersome and, for many anglers, easier to use.

The best electric motors are equipped with a device for modulating the pulse width. This conserves battery life, so the motor runs much longer on the same charge.

Another important accessory, especially for shallow-water fishing, is power trim. With a shallow-draft boat and power trim, you can motor through water only a foot deep. Power trim also improves your motor's high-speed performance.

Other handy, but not essential, accessories include lockable rod boxes and storage compartments, a bilge pump, a live well at least 48 inches long, an aerated bait well, a compass, and movable seats with extra pedestal bases. A drive-on trailer takes most of the work out of loading and unloading.

Useful Accessories for Pike-Muskie Boats

CASTING DECK. Make a removable deck by carpeting a piece of ¾-inch marine plywood cut to fit over your transom drain (left). Without a casting deck, an angler in the rear would stand too low to fish jerkbaits or see follows (right).

REMOVABLE SPLASH GUARDS. Splash guards keep you dry when you're backtrolling, but they're always in the way when casting. Splash guards that can be easily removed solve the problem; these attach with only two thumbscrews.

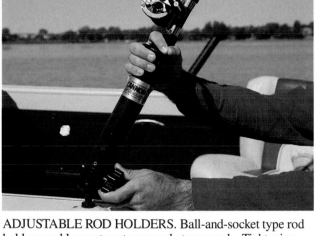

ADJUSTABLE ROD HOLDERS. Ball-and-socket type rod holders enable you to set your rod at any angle. Tightening the knob locks them securely in place. When you're not using them, they fold down on the gunwale, out of the way.

LOCKING ROD HOLDERS. This type works well for deep trolling, when you want your rod horizontal (left). Your rod cannot fall out, yet you can easily remove it when you get a strike (right).

MAKESHIFT BOW MOUNT. Loosen the head of a transom-mount troll motor, rotate it 180 degrees (top inset), then retighten it. This way, you can operate the motor in forward for maximum power. Attach the mounting bracket to the gunwale using a board as a spacer (bottom inset); adjust the tilt mechanism so the shaft of the motor is vertical.

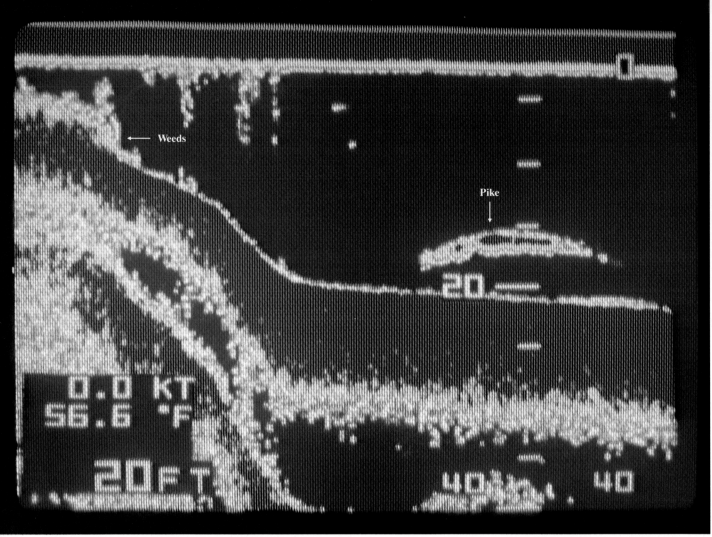

Weeds

Pike

0.0 KT
56.6 °F
20 FT
40 40

COLOR VIDEOS give you detailed information on what's below you. Not only do they have superior resolution, different colors mean different signal strengths, helping you determine fish size and bottom composition. This video screen shows a pike just off a weedline. The fish is easy to distinguish from the weeds.

Important Video Features

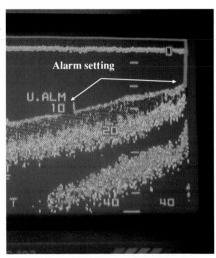

Alarm setting

U.ALM
10

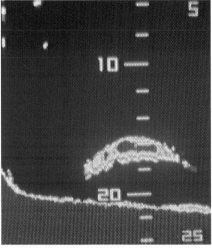

5

10

20

25

DUAL-CONE TRANSDUCERS enable you to switch from a wide cone, best when searching for fish, to a narrow cone, best for seeing fish when they're tight to the bottom.

DEPTH ALARMS are invaluable in lakes with lots of shallow reefs. The alarm warns you whenever the water is too shallow for safe navigation. This alarm is set to beep at 10 feet or less.

ZOOM capability allows you to expand the screen image. This is the same screen as in the large photo above, but only the 5- to 25-foot portion of the 0- to 40-foot range is displayed.

Electronics

Regardless of what kind of pike or muskie fishing you're doing, a depth finder is a must. If you're fishing shallow, all that's needed is a good flasher. It will help you follow the weedline and detect differences in bottom composition.

When pike or muskies are in deep water, either suspended or alongside cover, a graph is a big help. Select a liquid-crystal with good resolution (at least 160 vertical pixels) or, better yet, a video. Although videos are bulky and may be difficult to read in direct sunlight, they have the the best resolution and the fastest sweep speed – valuable assets, especially when you're searching for fish at high speed.

Although some anglers still prefer paper graphs, these units provide no more information than a good liquid-crystal or video. Another drawback: the paper is expensive, so you probably won't run the unit as much as you should.

A surface temperature gauge can help you find the fish, especially in spring when the sun warms the shallows and back bays. Some liquid-crystals and videos come with a temperature sensor built into the transducer. In summer, a hand-held temperature gauge that gives you a reading at any depth will help you locate coldwater pike (p. 119).

When you're trolling, a speed indicator enables you to maintain the speed that's best for the lure you're using. Some liquid-crystals and videos have speed indicators, but these devices may not be accurate enough at low speed. A separate trolling speed indicator will give you a more precise reading.

Another valuable tool is a Loran-C navigator, particularly when trolling for suspended fish in big water (p. 109). When you catch a fish, you can store the location in the unit's memory, then turn around and troll through the precise spot again. A marine radio is also a worthwhile big-water tool. It enables you to share fishing information with other anglers and call for help should boat problems arise.

Electronic gadgets such as pH meters and color selectors have not proven to be of value in pike and muskie fishing. In fact, they can mislead you into fishing in the wrong areas or using colors that have minimal appeal.

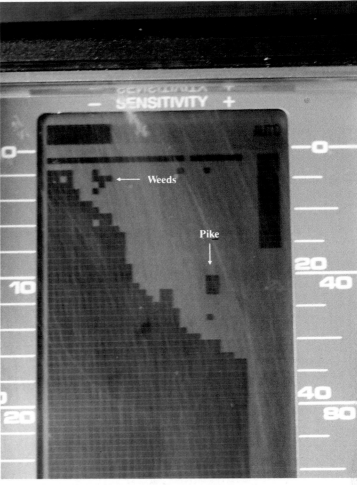

LOW-RESOLUTION LIQUID-CRYSTALS give you much less detail than a video. The clump of pixels on the left is actually weeds; the clump on the right, a pike. But the weeds look very much like the fish, and either mark could be a school of baitfish.

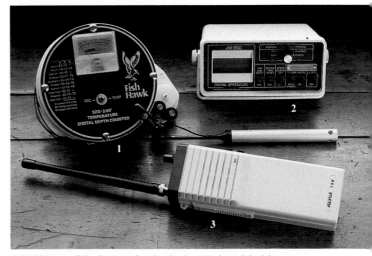

OTHER useful electronics include: (1) hand-held temperature gauge with a probe for measuring temperature in the depths; (2) trolling-speed indicator, for accurate readings at slow speed; and (3) hand-held marine radio, for sharing fishing information and for safety.

Other Equipment

Because of the large fish you're dealing with, and the bulky baits and lures used to catch them, pike-muskie fishing requires a fair amount of specialized equipment.

For instance, if you try to keep 10-inch suckers in a minnow bucket intended for crappie fishing, they'll die in minutes. You need a bucket that holds at least 5 gallons of water, preferably one with an aerator. In warm weather, use a cooler or other insulated container and add ice cubes periodically to keep the water cool.

You also need a large, sturdy net or a cradle (opposite page); special tools for unhooking the fish and cutting hooks; big tackle boxes that will keep your lures dry so the hooks don't rust; and sharpening devices that will handle large hooks.

TACKLE CONTAINERS for pike-muskie fishing include: (1) Plano Hanging Bait Box, (2) Bucktail Bag, (3) Northland Outdoors Lure Tube, (4) Styrofoam cooler and (5) Plano Phantom.

EQUIPMENT for landing and releasing fish includes: (1) landing net, with a sturdy hoop at least 30 inches in diameter and a deep bag; (2) cradle with built-in ruler, for landing and measuring fish you want to release; (3) jaw spreader;

(4) needlenose pliers, for cutting wire and removing hooks; (5) sidecutters, for cutting deeply embedded hooks; (6) club. for subduing fish you want to keep; and (7) Hook-out, for unhooking deeply hooked fish.

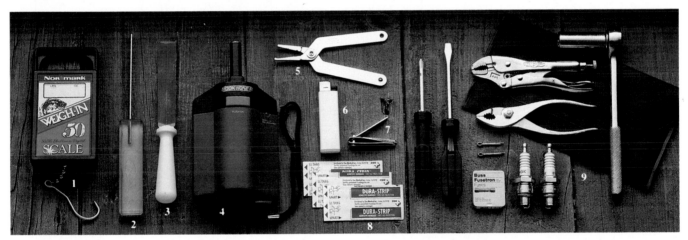

OTHER TOOLS include: (1) Normark 50-pound digital scale; (2) DMT diamond hook hone; (3) Luhr Jensen hook file; (4) Hook-Hone-R, a motorized hook sharpener; (5) split-ring pliers; (6) lighter, for making twist-melt connections

(p. 48) and splicing soft plastics (p. 71); (7) nail clipper, for cutting line; (8) adhesive bandages, for minor tooth cuts; (9) outboard tool kit with screwdrivers, wrenches, pliers, cotter keys, fuses and spark plugs.

BAIT CONTAINERS include: (1) Rex-Air 10-gallon aerated bucket, which operates on a 12-volt system; (2)

cooler with 12-volt aerator; (3) large floating mesh net, for keeping bait in the water overnight.

Basic Techniques for Pike & Muskies

Pike- & Muskie-Fishing Fundamentals

When a pike or muskie decides to take your bait, nothing will change its mind. These fish have been known to ram the boat when an angler lifts a lure from the water.

Because of their aggressive temperament, there's no need for a subtle presentation. You can use heavy line, a thick wire leader and big hooks. And if you splash your bait right on top of them, it's more likely to kindle their interest than to spook them.

Not that they're always willing biters. Pike rank among the easiest gamefish to catch, but muskies may well be the toughest. Even if you locate one, getting it to hit is another matter. They're notorious followers; some days, you'll see a dozen for every one that

strikes. The best way to turn followers into biters is to perfect your figure-eight technique (p. 60).

Pike and muskies have bony mouths, so sharp hooks are a must. But hooks large enough for these fish are usually quite dull when you buy them. It pays to carry a good sharpening device that will handle big hooks.

Landing a large Esocid requires the right tools and extreme care. If you stick your hand into its mouth or gills to free your hook, you risk serious injury from the teeth or gill rakers should the fish start thrashing.

Always carry jaw spreaders, a needlenose pliers and sidecutters for clipping off hooks. You can hand-land small pike and muskies (opposite page), but for big ones, you'll need a large net or, better yet, a cradle.

The strong catch-and-release ethic among dedicated muskie anglers has had a major impact in preserving quality muskie fishing. Carry a camera to document your catch, and keep a fish only if you plan to have it mounted. If you want fish to eat, take small pike.

How to Land Pike and Muskies

LAND a small pike or muskie by grabbing it firmly across the back, just behind the gill covers.

GRAB the tail of a played-out pike or muskie at boatside to prevent it from thrashing while another person frees the hooks. Never attempt to grab the tail if the fish is still "hot."

SLIDE a good-sized pike or muskie into a cradle if you plan to release it. A cradle restricts the fish's movement, preventing it from injuring itself and protecting you while you unhook it.

NET fish only if you plan to keep them. They may bruise themselves or split their fins in an ordinary landing net.

How to Unhook and Release Pike and Muskies

FREE hard-to-reach hooks with a long-handled hook remover. This way, you won't have to put your hand in the fish's mouth.

CUT the points off deeply embedded hooks using sidecutters. Then, you can get the fish back in the water quickly without injuring it.

HOLD the fish upright and gently rock it back and forth to revive it. Don't let the fish go unless it can remain upright on its own.

Figure-Eighting

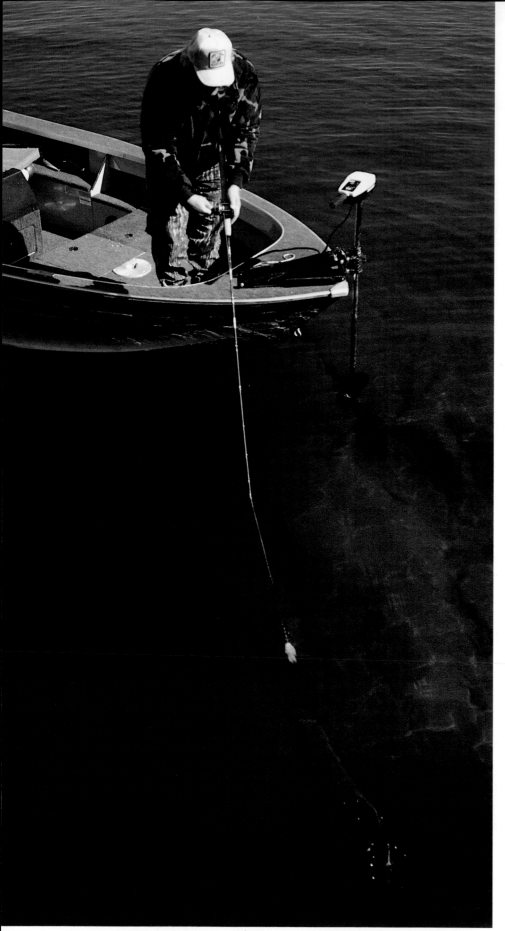

WATCH carefully for follows when retrieving your lure; polarized glasses and a long-billed cap are a must. If you're not paying attention, you may pull your lure away from a fish only inches behind it.

Figure-eighting works with most any kind of artificial lure, even top-waters and jerkbaits. Some muskie experts take up to 40 percent of their fish this way. The technique is effective for reluctant pike, too.

The idea behind the figure-eight technique is to keep the lure moving and try to keep it away from the fish by speeding it up. Most beginners use the opposite tactic; when a fish follows, they slow their retrieve or stop reeling altogether, causing the fish to lose interest.

Watch carefully to determine whether or not the fish is hot. If it's right on the lure and appears to be nipping at it, keep figure-eighting. But if it's swimming slowly and seems only mildly interested, leave it alone, mark the spot and come back a couple of hours later or when the weather changes. Or try again at dusk.

Figure-eighting is especially important in low-clarity water or at night, because you probably won't see your follows. In these situations, the best policy is to figure-eight, or at least make an L-turn, after every cast, just in case a fish is eyeing your lure.

It pays to figure-eight every few casts in clear water too; sometimes fish hang 3 or 4 feet beneath the boat and are tough to see.

The Figure-Eight Technique

EASE your rod tip under the surface when a fish follows. Draw the lure to within a foot of the tip, press the free-spool button and thumb the reel.

SWEEP the rod in a wide, smooth, figure-eight pattern, keeping the tip well below the bottom of the boat. If your pattern is too tight, a good-sized fish won't be able to turn sharply enough to follow the lure. If the fish won't come up for the lure, push the lure deeper.

TRIGGER a strike from a half-interested fish by drawing the lure across its snout. Do not use this technique if the fish is hot.

SET THE HOOK when you feel the weight of the fish. Your hooking percentage is best when you set upward or back into the fish.

Fishing Pike & Muskies with Artificial Lures

When you see a big, shadowy form inches behind your lure, you'll understand why so many anglers fish pike and muskies with artificials. Bait fishermen rarely experience the thrill of seeing a follow, then figure-eighting to make the fish strike.

Almost anything with a hook attached will catch pike and muskies – when they're in the right mood. But when they're not, lure selection becomes critical. Following are the main considerations in deciding what artificials to use:

SIZE. When we discussed food habits (p. 16), we said that pike and muskies preferred baitfish at least one-fourth their own length. If you follow this line of reasoning, a 48-inch muskie, which weighs about 30 pounds, would be more likely to strike a foot-long lure than the 4- to 6-inchers used by most anglers.

But 30-pounders are scarce in most waters; if you relied solely on foot-long lures, you wouldn't get many strikes. Gauge the size of your lure to the size of the fish you expect to catch. If your lake has plenty of 5-pounders, for instance, but seldom produces a 10, a 7- to 8-inch lure would be a better choice. Go a little smaller in spring or after a cold front, a little larger in fall.

RUNNING DEPTH. Being aggressive predators, pike and muskies may swim up 10 to 20 feet to take a lure. But when they're not in the mood to feed, you'll have to put it right in their face. It's a good idea to carry a selection of lures that run at different depths, from the surface down to 30 feet.

Another suggestion: carry a variety of pinch-on or twist-on sinkers so you can weight your lures to go deeper. With some, such as bucktails and spinnerbaits, you can add weight to the lure itself; with others, you'll have to attach the weight just ahead of the lure.

If you're not sure how deep a lure runs, find an area with a clean, gradually sloping bottom. Then make a long cast and retrieve the lure at normal speed. If you don't feel it hit bottom, move shallower until

you do. Write the running depth on the lure with waterproof ink.

Many pike and muskie anglers make the mistake of using line much heavier than what's really needed.

The water resistance of thick-diameter line lifts the lure, preventing it from reaching its depth potential. Thus a lure that runs 8 feet deep with 30-pound mono may run 12 feet deep with 17-pound.

ACTION. As a rule, the intensity of the action should increase as the season progresses. In spring, lures with a tight wobble or subtle action usually work best. By fall, however, the fish seem to prefer lures that have a wider wobble or more erratic action, those that make lots of noise and splash or those with hard-thumping blades. Lures with high-intensity action also work well in low-clarity waters.

When casting, it pays to vary your retrieve to change the lure's action. Speed up, slow down, give it a twitch now and then and switch your rod from side to side to change direction. When trolling, sweep your rod forward every few seconds, then drop it back. If a fish is following, the hesitation often draws a strike. But at night or in murky water, use a steady retrieve; it's harder for the fish to home in on a lure moving erratically, so they'll often miss it.

COLOR. For decades, the accepted color for pike was red-and-white; for muskies, black. And no doubt those colors produced the most fish since few anglers used anything else. Today, serious fishermen carry a large assortment of different-colored lures for waters of different clarity and different weather conditions. The chart at right provides some general guidelines to color selection for pike and muskie fishing. There's no need to make a distinction between the two species. Following these recommendations will improve your odds – most of the time.

But remember that there are no hard-and-fast rules. Stick with colors that you know have produced in the body of water you're fishing, but don't hesitate to experiment if they're not working.

Color-Selection Chart

	CLEAR TO MODERATELY CLEAR WATER		LOW-CLARITY WATER (visibility of 2 feet or less)	
Spinner-blade Color	Nickel (C, O) Gold or Brass (C, O) Fluorescent Orange (O) Fluorescent Chartreuse (O)		Gold or Brass (C) Copper (C) Fluorescent Orange (C, O) Fluorescent Chartreuse (C, O)	
Lure or Bucktail Color	Black (C, O) Brown (C, O) Purple (C, O) Gray (C, O) White (C, O)	Silver (C, O) Gold (O) Red (O) Fluorescent Chartreuse (O)	Black (C, O) Yellow (C, O) White (C, O) Fluorescent Orange (C, O) Fluorescent Chartreuse (C, O)	Gold (C) Copper (C)

COLOR SELECTION depends on water clarity and cloud cover. Good colors for waters of high to moderate clarity are listed in the left column; low clarity, in the right.

Spinner-blade colors are listed at the top; lure-body or bucktail colors, at the bottom. The letter "C" signifies a good choice for clear skies; "O," overcast skies.

Fishing with Bucktails and Spinnerbaits

most often used for casting, but also work well for trolling.

Circumstances dictate whether to use a bucktail or a spinnerbait.

BUCKTAILS. The term *bucktail* has been applied loosely to any large in-line spinner, regardless of the type of tail dressing. But the best bucktails are actually dressed with hair from a deer tail. Because deer hair is hollow, it is very buoyant and has an attractive billowing or breathing action in the water. The deer hair is usually tied around the base of a treble hook at the rear. Some baits have two or even three dressed trebles in a line.

The big, thumping blades on these spinners produce enough vibration to attract pike and muskies from a distance, even in low-clarity water where they can barely see.

Though generally consided to be warmwater lures, spinners will catch fish in cool water too, if you slow down your retrieve.

Spinners can be retrieved quite rapidly, so they enable you to cover a lot of water in a hurry. They're

In water with few weeds or other obstructions, a bucktail is a better choice than a spinnerbait. Normally, you fish this lure with a straight retrieve, so pike and muskies have no trouble zeroing in on it. This quality, combined with the exposed treble(s) at

BUCKTAIL models include: (1) single-blade, such as Windel's Harasser, by far the most common type; and (2) tandem-blade, such as the Com Boo, which has more flash and better lift.

SPINNERBAIT models include: (1) single-blade, such as the Eagle Spin, best for fishing in deep water and helicoptering; and (2) tandem-blade, such as the M-G spinnerbait, best for bulging because of the extra lift.

the rear, results in a hooking percentage higher than that of most other lures.

When casting bucktails, start reeling just as the lure hits the water. If you let it sink, the hook may foul on the line. Reel rapidly at first to get the blade spinning. If it starts, you'll feel the vibrations. If it doesn't, give the lure a sharp twitch. Then slow down; the blade will keep spinning.

The main considerations when selecting bucktails are size and running depth. In spring, when the water is below 60° F, use a 3- to 5-inch-long bucktail. Later, use 6- to 10-inchers. Bigger bucktails also seem to work better in low-clarity water and at night. For trophy fishing, or when hammer-handle northerns are a problem, don't be afraid to try bucktails as long as 12 inches.

How deep you want your bucktail to run depends mainly on the water depth or the depth at which the weeds top out. As a rule, if that depth is less than 5 feet, use a shallow runner; greater than 5 feet, a deep runner.

Running depth can be gauged as follows: the lighter the body, the more hair or soft-plastic dressing, and the larger and rounder the blade, the shallower the lure will track (p. 66). Also, a tandem-blade bucktail will run shallower than a single.

You can regulate the depth at which a bucktail tracks by simply changing your retrieve speed. When you speed up, the blade spins more rapidly, creating more "lift" and making the lure run shallower. If you hold your rod tip high and reel fast, even a deep runner will "bulge" the surface, making a wake that often draws the fishes' attention.

SPINNERBAITS. Because the safety-pin shaft "runs interference" for the single upturned hook, a spinnerbait will go through most heavy weeds without fouling. The blade is attached to a swivel, so it spins not only when the lure is pulled forward, but also when it sinks. The lead head makes the lure sink rapidly and acts as a keel, preventing line twist. But spinnerbaits have one drawback: the single hook reduces your hooking percentage. If you'll be fishing in open water, it pays to use a spinnerbait with a treble-hook trailer.

A spinnerbait is one of the most versatile pike-muskie lures. You can cast or troll it over shallow, weedy flats, "helicopter" it into holes in or alongside the weeds, jig it along bottom, bulge it on the surface as you would a bucktail or count it down to reach suspended fish.

Like bucktails, spinnerbaits come in single- or tandem-blade models. Singles run deeper, helicopter better and have less wind resistance, so they're easier to cast. But tandems produce more vibration, an advantage in murky water or at night. Spinnerbaits with willow-leaf blades are most weedless because the blade spins closest to the shaft. Most good spinnerbaits have thick wire shafts; those with thinner wire bend easily but vibrate more.

In spring, use $\frac{1}{4}$- to $\frac{3}{8}$-ounce bass spinnerbaits. In summer and fall, you'll probably do better on $\frac{1}{2}$- to 1-ounce sizes. Weight, dressing and blade size affect the running depth of spinnerbaits in the same way they do bucktails.

Lures shown ¾ actual size

RUNNING DEPTH of bucktails is determined by blade type, body weight and tail bulk. The top lure runs shallowest because it has a fluted Indiana blade, a body made of hollow beads and a bulky tandem tail. The middle lure runs deeper due to the French-style blade, the bullet-type body and the thinner tandem tail. The bottom lure runs deepest because of the willow-leaf blade, the solid-brass body and the single tail.

Bucktail Tips

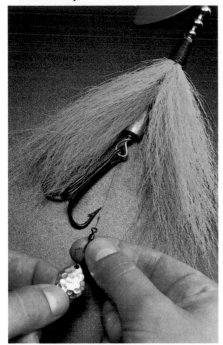

ADD a teaser by haywire-twisting 2 or 3 inches of single-strand wire to the loop of wire holding the rear hook and to a snap-swivel. Clip a small spinner blade to the swivel.

REPLACE the blade if it doesn't spin at the start of the retrieve. A thin blade (left) may plane too much; a thick one (right) hangs vertically, so it catches water and starts to turn.

CHANGE blades quickly by cutting the metal next to the hole as shown, replacing the old blade with a new one, then bending the metal to close the cut. The blade will not come off.

Spinnerbait Tips

BULGE a spinnerbait by holding your rod tip high and reeling fast enough so the blades almost, but not quite, break the surface. Bulging works best when the fish are active.

PINCH a dog-ear-style sinker onto the lower shaft of a spinnerbait for extra depth. Or, using a split ring, attach a bell sinker to the eye of the rear hook.

TIP a spinnerbait with a live minnow for extra attraction. Hook the minnow through the head. Don't use minnows more than 4 inches long or you'll get too many short strikes.

The slow, tantalizing action of a jig appeals to pike and muskies anytime, but jigs really outshine other lures when fishing gets tough.

In early spring, for instance, muskies are seldom caught until the water temperature rises above 40. But many an early-season walleye angler has been startled by a huge muskie cruising up and inhaling his jig. Another good time for jig fishing is late fall, when the rapidly cooling water slows pike and muskie activity. Jigs work well after a cold front, in calm, sunny weather and in ultraclear lakes.

A jig is also a good choice for thoroughly working a tight spot, such as an inside turn in a deep weedline. When you're casting bucktails, crankbaits or other "fast" lures, you'll see lots of fish that won't strike. Rather than pester them with the same lure, leave them alone for a while, then come back and toss a jig.

The proper weight and style of jig depends on the water depth and type of cover. Most pike-muskie jigs have a large, buoyant body, so the head must be heavier than that of a smaller-bodied jig used for bass or walleyes.

Here's a good rule of thumb regarding jig weight: use a ⅜-ounce head in water 10 feet or shallower; add ⅛ ounce for each additional 5 feet. If you're fishing in current or strong wind, choose a slightly heavier jig.

When fishing in weeds, use a pyramid-style jig head. The tapered shape and attachment eye at the front allow the jig to slide through most vegetation without fouling. Few pike-muskie jigs come with a weedguard; if you need one, make your own (p. 71) or use a weedless bass jig and add a soft-plastic eel-tail, curly tail or creature.

POPULAR JIGS for pike-muskie fishing include: (1) shad-tails, such as Jack's 9" Rigged Shad; (2) eel-tails, such as the Mar-Lyn Reaper on a pyramid-head jig; (3) spin-tails, such as the Curtis Creature; (4) swimmer-head

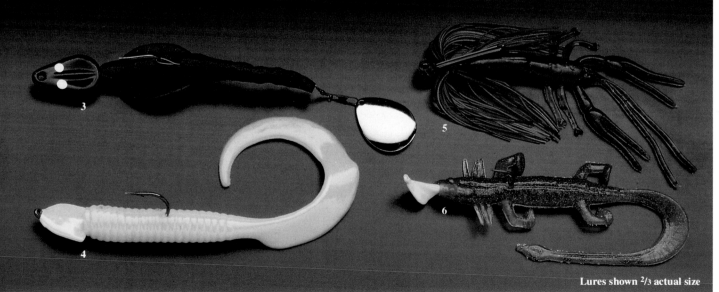

Lures shown ²/₃ actual size

jigs, such as Jack's Swimmer Head rigged with a curly tail; (5) brushguard jigs, such as the Stanley Jig with a Guido Bug trailer; and (6) creatures, such as Mann's Auger Lizard on a pyramid-head jig.

If you're fishing in deep water with a clean bottom, a ball-head jig is a better choice than a pyramid head because it gets down faster. In shallow water or in dense weeds that grow nearly to the surface, a swimmer head is ideal because you can keep it riding high at a slow retrieve speed.

Whatever type of jig you select, it should have a forged hook. Some anglers prefer wire hooks for fishing in woody cover (p. 106), but wire may straighten from the weight of a big fish.

Pike and muskies find it hard to resist soft-plastic dressings such as curly tails, creatures and shad. Soft plastics have a realistic look and a lifelike action, and they sink slowly, giving the fish plenty of time to strike. But plastic bodies tend to slip down the hook shank. Add a drop of super glue to the collar of your jig to hold soft plastics securely.

Another popular dressing is bucktail. The hollow hairs also sink slowly, and they give the lure an undulating, or breathing, action. Try to find jigs with hair at least 3 inches long.

The principles of color selection that apply to other artificial lures (p. 63) also apply to jigs. However, some veteran pike anglers swear by red jig heads, regardless of when or where they're fishing.

There's no right or wrong way to work a jig, but the colder the water, the slower and less erratic your retrieve should be. In early spring, the best technique may be simply to cast the jig, let it sink to the bottom, then inch it back slowly and steadily, or with hops of no more than a few inches. But in midsummer, "rip-jigging" may work better. Retrieve rapidly with sharp jerks, keeping the jig a foot or two off bottom and letting it settle back on a slack line between jerks. Experiment with different jigging motions and retrieve speeds until you find the combination that works best for the conditions.

The secret to successful jig fishing is learning to detect subtle strikes. When the fish are active, they slam the jig, but there are times when strikes are nearly imperceptible. All you feel is a slight tick or maybe the jig just stops sinking. Always use a sensitive rod, keep your line taut as the jig sinks and set the hook whenever you feel anything out of the ordinary.

When the fish are fussy, try tipping your jig with suckers, chubs, smelt, ciscoes or even waterdogs. The bait doesn't have to be alive; in fact, live-bait anglers commonly ice down any baitfish that die, then use them later for tipping jigs.

Don't tip your jig with any bait longer than 6 inches; you'll get too many short hits. If you have this problem, add a stinger hook (see below) or try hesitating for a few seconds when you feel a pickup. Pike and muskies aren't likely to spit the jig, and giving them more time will improve your hooking percentage.

How to Tip a Jig with Live Bait

PUSH (1) the hook through the mouth of a 4-inch minnow and out just behind the head. (2) Hook a 5- to 6-inch minnow through the lips and insert one prong of the stinger hook ahead of the tail. The stinger is attached to a piece of 20-pound stainless-steel wire haywire-twisted (p. 48) to the bend of the jig hook. Rig a waterdog with a stinger just as you would a large minnow; insert the treble behind the rear leg.

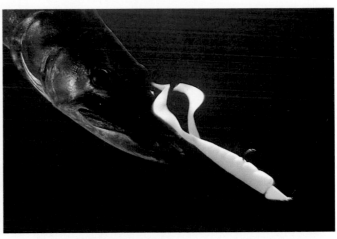

WATCH closely for followers (left). If you spot one, stop reeling, open the bail or push the free-spool button and let your jig free-fall (right). This tactic is more likely to draw a strike than figure-eighting.

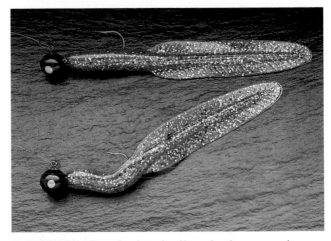

FLATTEN a ball-head jig to make it a swimmer head. Place the jig head in a vice open just enough so the attachment eye can slip between the jaws. Pound the jig with a hammer to achieve the desired shape.

OVERTHREAD a plastic eel-tail to give it more action. Normally, the tail is hooked so it trails straight (top). Pushing the hook farther through the tail (bottom) adds a slight bend, giving the tail more wiggle.

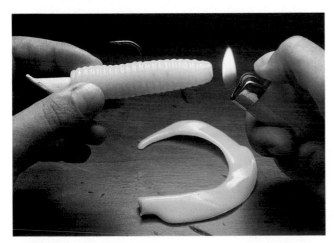

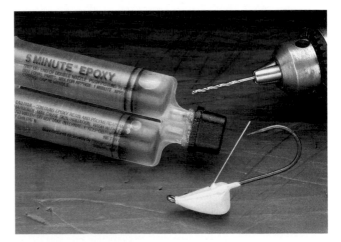

REPAIR a tooth-severed creature or other soft plastic by melting one end with a lighter, then pressing the ends back together. You can also use this technique to make a "firetail" or other multicolor pattern.

MAKE a brushguard for your jig by drilling a small hole in the jig head just to the side of the hook shank, inserting a piece of stiff-wire leader as shown and securing it with epoxy glue. Bend the wire as needed to protect the hook point.

LOOK for a telltale bulge from 6 inches to 2 feet behind your lure; it means a fish is following. If the fish is hot, its back or tail may break the surface. When you see a follower, reel faster. Most anglers make the mistake of slowing down to let the fish catch the lure, but when they do, the fish loses interest.

Fishing with Topwater Lures

If the thought of an explosive surface strike gets your blood boiling, try fishing pike and muskies with topwater lures.

Once the water temperature hits 60° F in spring, topwaters begin to produce; they continue to catch fish through early fall. They work best in shallow water (12 feet or less) and in overcast weather with no more than a slight chop. When the water gets rough, the fish may not notice the lure unless it makes a lot of surface disturbance.

Topwaters are ideal for fishing over dense weedbeds where most other lures would foul. Pike and muskies are accustomed to swimming up to attack frogs, mice, ducklings and injured baitfish.

Muskie anglers rely heavily on topwaters for night fishing. The best lures produce a lot of noise with a slow retrieve. Muskies have an even tougher time zeroing in on a fast-moving lure at night than during the day.

One problem with topwaters: you'll probably miss more fish than with other artificials.

The fish often strike just behind the moving lure, making a good-sized swirl or splash, which causes you to set the hook. But when you set, you pull the lure away from the fish. If you can hold off, it will probably hit the lure again. Never set the hook until you feel the weight of the fish.

The most common mistake in using topwaters is retrieving too rapidly. The faster you reel, the more strikes you miss. Small fish are more inclined to

PROPBAITS for pike-muskie fishing include: (1) twin-prop models, such as the Stidham Muskie Probe, with propeller blades front and rear; (2) head-spins, such as the Bauer Chippewa; (3) tail-spins, such as the Mud Puppy; and (4) double tail-spins, such as the Hi-Fin Twin Teaser-tail, which have the most intense action.

Lures shown ²/₃ actual size

chase a fast-moving surface lure; bigger ones prefer a slower retrieve. Another frequent error: using a heavy leader. A thick wire leader with heavy hardware weights the nose of a topwater so much that it plows water and loses action.

If a fish follows your topwater to the boat, don't figure-eight on the surface. Instead, draw the lure underwater and figure-eight as you would with a sub-surface lure (p. 61).

Topwaters come in many different designs that produce different sounds and actions. Following are the most popular types:

PROPBAITS. These lures have propellers at one or both ends. Sometimes the head or tail spins along with the propeller, throwing more water and creating more commotion than a propeller by itself.

In clear or calm water, propbaits with a subdued action work better than those with a violent action. But in low-clarity water, on a choppy surface or at night, the reverse is usually true.

Most often, propbaits are retrieved slowly and steadily, with periodic twitches mixed in. But when you're scouting, reel a little faster. You'll miss more fish, but you'll see where they are so you can try them again later.

BUZZBAITS. Some have a safety-pin shaft, like a spinnerbait; others, a straight, in-line shaft, like a bucktail spinner. One or two double- or triple-winged propellers churn the surface.

In-line buzzers have a treble hook instead of a single, so they hook fish better. But the safety-pin types are much less likely to foul in weeds.

Buzzbaits, especially the in-line type, are light, making them harder to cast than other surface lures. Their silhouette is smaller, so they're not the best choice for night fishing. But you can retrieve them

Lures shown ¹/₂ actual size

BUZZBAITS include: (1) single-spins, such as the Strike King Cackle Buzz; (2) double-spins, such as the Blue Fox Double Buzzer; and (3) in-line buzzers, such as the Buchertail Tandem Buzzer.

faster than other topwaters, so they're excellent "locator" lures.

CRAWLERS. These stocky plugs have arms on each side or a cupped face or lip that produces a wide wobble and a loud, gurgling sound when fished with a slow, steady retrieve. If you reel too fast, the lure won't catch enough water and will plane on the surface.

Because of their slow, straight action, crawlers hook fish better than most other topwaters. Their action also makes them a good choice for fishing muskies at night, particularly in areas where you've spotted fish during the day.

Figure-eighting is more difficult with crawlers than with other topwaters. They tend to roll when you draw them under. Instead, try to make the fish hit on the surface by giving the lure several sharp twitches.

STICKBAITS. These long, slender surface plugs have little action of their own. But a series of rapid, downward twitches gives them an enticing side-to-side action. This erratic retrieve is called "walking-the-dog."

Because stickbaits do not have blades, arms or lips to throw water, their action is not as intense as most other topwaters, making it harder for fish to home in on them. Consequently, they're most often used in relatively clear water.

Most effective, over submerged weedbeds, stickbaits are not a good choice for fishing in emergents because the side-to-side action tends to catch the stems. Another drawback: the erratic action results in many missed strikes.

Lures shown ¹/₂ actual size

CRAWLERS include: (1) arm-type models, such as the Hi-Fin Creeper; (2) cup-faced models, such as the Musky Jitterbug; and (3) cup-lipped models, such as the Hawg Wobbler.

Lure shown ¹/₂ actual size

TYPICAL STICKBAIT - Poe's Giant Jackpot

The Getaway Technique

CAST a buzzbait, let it sink a little, and with your rod down, reel slowly enough that the lure tracks just beneath the surface (left). As it approaches the boat, speed up your retrieve and raise your rod, drawing the lure to the surface. As the blades begin to break water (right), followers strike so their prey doesn't "get away."

Topwater Tips

CUP buzzbait-style blades to make them throw more water. Using a needlenose pliers, bend in the ends of the blades more than they already are.

BEND the fin on a tail-spin propbait if it won't spin properly. The blade on a new lure (left) may not be bent enough. It should make a right angle to the lure's centerline (right).

DRAW the lure under if you see a fish following. Push your rod tip down, reel the lure to within a foot of the tip, then start to figure-eight.

SET THE HOOK sideways when using topwaters. With the lure tracking on the surface, an upward set could send the lure flying back at you if you miss.

CRANKBAITS for pike-muskie fishing include: (1) shallow runners, such as the Rapala Fat Rap; (2) deep runners, such as the Bagley DB-06; and (3) extra-deep runners, such as the Whopper Stopper Hellbender.

Fishing with Subsurface Plugs

Practically every longtime pike or muskie hound has an old, beat-up plug that is perforated with teeth marks, a reminder of past Esocid encounters.

The following categories of subsurface plugs differ considerably in action, but all are effective for pike and muskies. These plugs differ from jerkbaits (p. 80) because they wobble or vibrate when retrieved.

CRANKBAITS. The front lip gives these lures an intense wobble. Most crankbaits float at rest, which is a definite advantage when you're fishing over weeds or logs. When you feel the lure bumping an obstruction, stop reeling and it will float back up. If you hook a weed, a sharp jerk of the rod will often rip the lure free.

How deep a crankbait runs depends on the size and angle of its lip. Some dive only a few feet; others, as much as 30. As a rule, a crankbait will run twice as deep when you're trolling as when you're casting. Some crankbaits sink, so you can count them down to fish in deep water.

MINNOW PLUGS. The effectiveness of these lures is partly due to their shape. Esocids and most other predator fish prefer long, slim baitfish because they're easy to swallow.

Minnow plugs work well for casting or trolling. They have a tighter, more lifelike wobble than crankbaits. But many anglers prefer to retrieve them in jerkbait fashion to create a tantalizing stop-and-go action. When the fish aren't aggressive, try twitching a minnow plug or crankbait on the surface (p. 79).

Like crankbaits, minnow plugs come in floating and sinking models. Floaters run anywhere from a few to more than 15 feet deep. Sinkers can be counted down to any depth.

MINNOW PLUGS include: (1) shallow-running floaters, such as the Bagley 8" Bang-O-Lure; (2) deep-running floaters, such as the Bomber Diving Long A; and (3) sinkers, such as the Countdown Rapala Magnum.

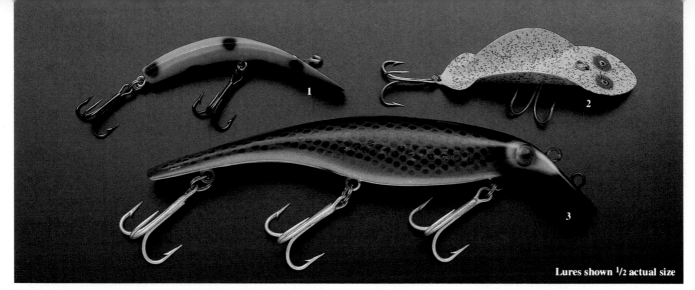

Lures shown ¹/₂ actual size

TROLLING PLUGS include: (1) shallow runners, such as a Flatfish, with the attachment eye near the snout; and (2) deep runners, such as a Spoonplug, with the attachment

eye farther back from the snout. Some plugs, such as a (3) Believer, have separate attachment eyes for deep and shallow running.

Most minnow plugs are plastic, but many anglers prefer those made of balsa wood because their wobble is more intense. However, some balsa plugs are too light to cast well, especially against a stiff wind, and they won't stand up to the sharp teeth of Esocids.

When selecting balsa minnow plugs for pike and muskies, make sure the hooks are anchored well to the plug body. Some models have an internal wire that prevents the hooks from pulling out of the soft wood.

TROLLING PLUGS. These lures have a flattened or scooped-out forehead that makes them difficult to cast but produces an extra-wide wobble. Different models run at different depths, from 2 feet to 20.

Trolling over large, shallow flats or along lengthy weedlines is a good way to locate pike and muskies. Once you find them, switch to casting to cover the area more thoroughly.

Some plugs are designed for slow trolling, others for speed trolling (p. 105). If you troll too fast with a slow-trolling plug, it spins or skates to the surface. Speed-trolling plugs, on the other hand, don't have much action at slow speed. To find the right speed for the plug you're using, let out a few feet of line and run the plug alongside the boat.

VIBRATING PLUGS. With the attachment eye on the back, these lures have a tight wiggle and produce high-frequency vibrations that fish can detect even in muddy water.

Most vibrating plugs sink, but some float. Sinkers are most versatile because you can cast them and count them down to the desired depth or troll them, increasing depth by letting out more line. Floating models work well over shallow weed flats. All vibrating plugs catch fewer weeds than plugs with lips.

For the best action, attach all subsurface plugs with a round-nosed snap or clip on a thin, braided-wire leader. A heavy snap-swivel or thick-wire leader will restrict the wobble too much.

To achieve maximum depth, all subsurface plugs must run perfectly straight. If they veer to one side or the other, they're "out of tune." To tune them, simply bend the attachment eye or the wire attachment arm to the opposite side.

Line diameter also affects the running depth of subsurface plugs. Thin line has less water resistance, so your lure will track deeper than with thick line. The smaller the plug, the more line diameter affects its running depth.

Lures shown actual size

VIBRATING PLUGS include: (1) floating models, such as a Rat-l-Trap Floater, and (2) sinkers, such as a Rattl'n

Rap. Most of these lures have internal lead shot that makes a rattling noise in addition to adding weight.

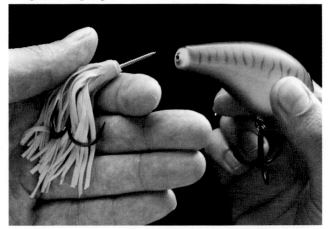

ADD a rubber skirt to a plug for more action. Remove the rear hook, thread on the skirt and replace the hook.

PAUSE a few seconds after twitching a floating minnow plug or crankbait, allowing it to float back to the surface. Then twitch it again to make it dive. A half-interested fish usually strikes when the lure is at rest.

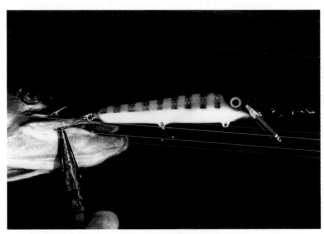

REPLACE the rear treble with a single Siwash hook and remove the front treble when you're catching lots of fish. You'll be able to unhook them much faster, and you're less likely to injure them.

SELECT plugs with sturdy lips such as the (1) Grandma, which has an extra-thick, strongly anchored Lexan lip, and the (2) Bagley DB-06, which has a wire connecting the lip to the body.

USE a metal-lipped plug when fishing on a rocky bottom. Rocks may break thin plastic lips (inset) or knock them completely off. Even if the lip stays intact, the rocks will gouge it, causing the lure to track to the side.

A touch of color can make a difference

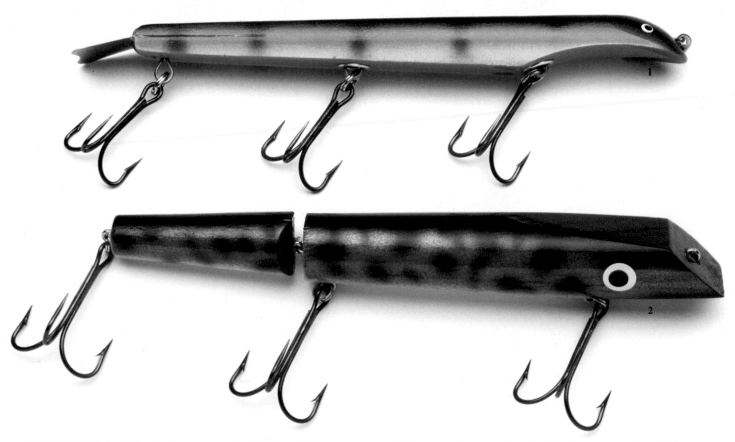

DIVERS include: (1) tailbaits, such as the Suick, which have a metal tail that can be bent to change the dive angle; and (2) true divers, such as the Stidham Sensor, in which the angle of the head determines how it dives.

Jerkbait Fishing

These big wooden plugs have no built-in action. They do only what you make them do. When retrieved with a series of sharp jerks, they dart erratically, like an injured baitfish. This action often appeals to pike and muskies more than a regular wobbling action.

Although jerkbaits vary widely in size, shape and action, they fall into two main categories: divers, which dart downward when pulled forward; and gliders, which swing from side to side with each pull.

Divers run 2 to 4 feet deeper than gliders, so they're a better choice for working deep water. They also work better in dense weeds. They have very little side-to-side movement, so you can thread them through narrow slots in the vegetation. But there are times when the fish prefer the erratic lateral action of a glider.

Most jerkbaits float at rest, but some anglers add weight to make the lures less buoyant (p. 83). Extra weight not only makes a jerkbait run deeper, but also allows you to work it more slowly. Because it takes longer for the lure to float up after each jerk, you don't have to retrieve as fast to hold the depth.

Missed strikes are a common problem when fishing jerkbaits, especially gliders. Because of their erratic action, the fish have a hard time zeroing in on them. And when a fish grabs a jerkbait, it sometimes sinks its teeth into the wood, making it difficult to move the plug enough to set the hook.

Despite their large size and lack of built-in action, jerkbaits can be figure-eighted in much the same manner as bucktails, spoons or crankbaits. Just add some short twitches while you make the figure-eight pattern.

Lures shown 2/3 actual size

GLIDERS include: (1) flashbaits, such as the Bagley B-Flat, which have an erratic action; and (2) true gliders, such as the Eddie Bait, which have a regular side-to-side gliding motion.

81

DIVER. Point your rod at the lure and sweep it smoothly downward to make the lure dive (inset). Stop the rod at 6 o'clock. Reel up slack while returning the rod to the original position. Continue retrieving with a series of sweeps; how long you hesitate between sweeps determines how deep the lure will track.

GLIDER. Point your rod tip at the lure and make a 6- to 18-inch downward twitch. The lure will glide to one side (inset). Reel up the slack and twitch again before the lure finishes its glide to make it veer the other way. If you wait too long, the lure may not change direction. Continue retrieving with short, rhythmic twitches.

How to Weight a Jerkbait

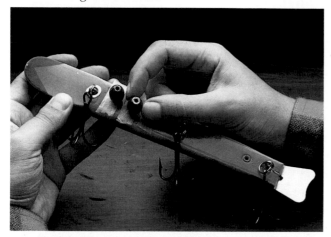

1. ATTACH several egg sinkers to the bottom of a jerkbait using small pieces of carpet tape, which has adhesive on both sides.

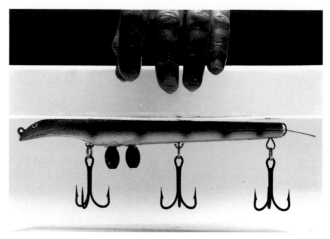

2. TEST the lure's buoyancy by floating it in water. Add enough sinkers so the lure barely floats. It should ride in a horizontal position.

3. DRILL a sinker-size hole at the exact spot each sinker was taped. Wrap masking tape around the drill bit to serve as a depth gauge.

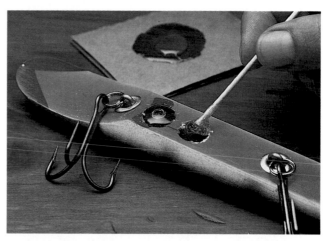

4. INSERT the egg sinkers into the holes, then fill the holes with epoxy glue. Allow the glue to dry for at least an hour before submerging the lure.

Quick Weighting Methods

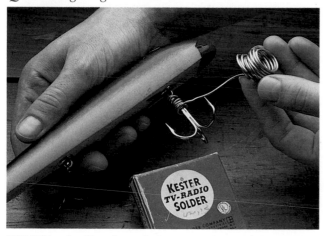

WRAP lead solder through the eye and around the shank of your jerkbait hooks until the lure floats with its back just out of the water.

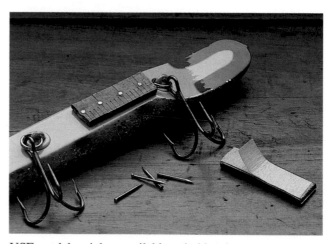

USE model weights, available at hobby shops, to weight a jerkbait. They have adhesive on one side, so you can move them to achieve the right balance. Tack them in place.

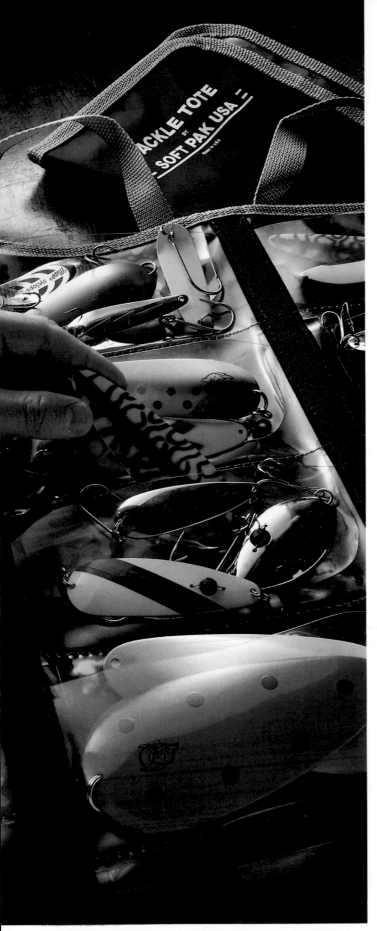

Spoon Fishing

Only a few decades ago, spoons were about the only lure anyone tossed at pike and muskies. And even though spoons play a lesser role in Esocid angling today, they still catch plenty of fish.

The usual way to fish a spoon is simply to retrieve or troll it at a steady pace. But spoon-fishing experts know that's not the whole story. Spoons can also be fished with an erratic stop-and-go retrieve, ripped over the weed tops, fluttered into pockets or along edges of the weeds, vertically jigged in deeper water and even skittered across the surface like a topwater.

Most pike-muskie spoons measure from 4 to 6 inches long. A wide assortment is available, ranging from thin models for maximum wobble to thick models for distance casting and vertical jigging to weedless models for thick cover. Weedless spoons work best when coupled with a pork strip, plastic curly tail or other attractor.

You don't need expensive spoons to catch pike and muskies. Any spoon will work, as long as the hooks are strong and sharp.

For the best action, clip the spoon to a thin, braided-wire leader. A stiff leader restricts the wobble too much. Many anglers prefer a single Siwash hook (p . 79) to a treble because it provides more positive hook sets and makes it easier to release fish unharmed.

Spoon-Fishing Tips

STORE your spoons in a soft pack for longer life. Stacking them in the trays of an ordinary tackle box chips the paint and dulls the metal.

SKITTER a spoon on the surface by keeping your rod tip high as you retrieve. The spoon should ride with the convex side down.

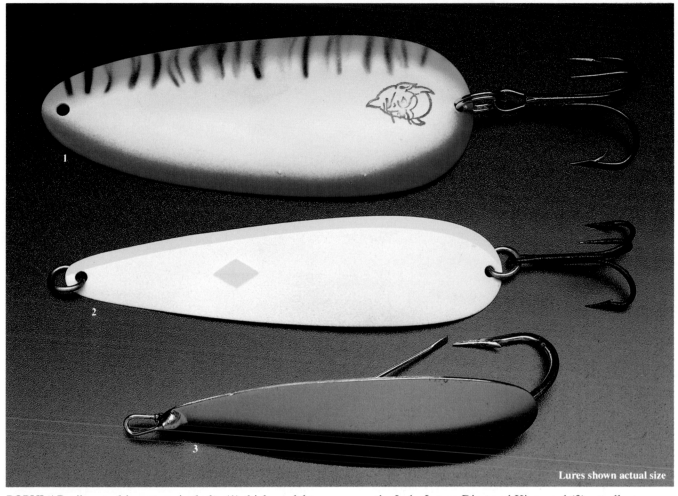

POPULAR pike-muskie spoons include: (1) thick models, such as the Eppinger Husky-Devle; (2) thin models, such as the Luhr Jensen Diamond King; and (3) weedless models, such as the Johnson Silver Minnow.

IMPROVE a spoon's action by adding a split ring to the front eye (left) and a soft-plastic or pork-rind trailer to the hook (right).

RESTORE the shine to old spoons using metal polish or fine steel wool. Some types of metal polish, however, will dissolve paint. Test them before application.

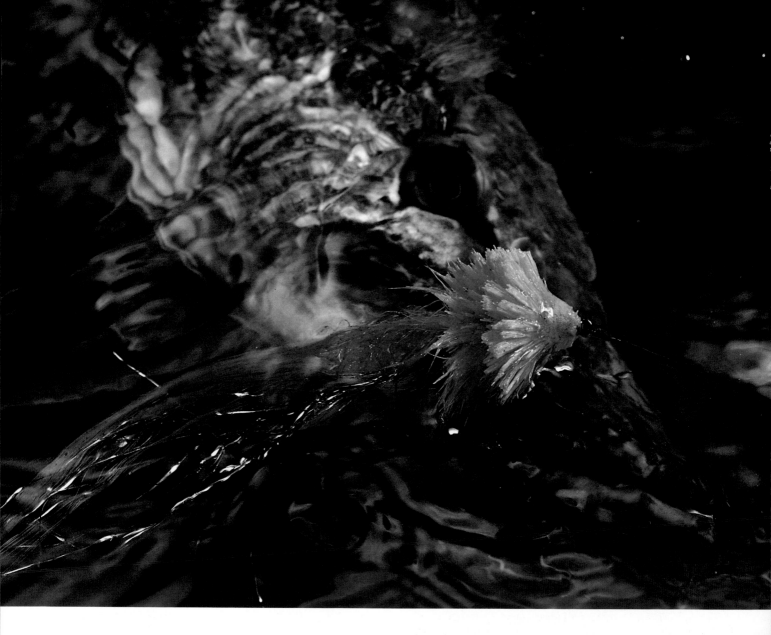

Fly Fishing

Landing a big pike or muskie on a fly rod ranks among the top thrills in freshwater fishing. But very little has been written on the subject, and many fly shops don't carry the right flies.

The most effective flies include streamers, crayfish and frog imitations, poppers, divers and weighted rabbit-fur flies.

Depending on the size of the fish you expect to catch, select flies in sizes 2 to 4/0. Flies tied with a little tinsel produce more flash and generally draw more strikes. A stiff wire or mono weedguard is a must when fishing in weeds, brush or logs.

Many anglers believe that flycasting is strictly a technique for shallow water, but with a full-sinking line and weighted fly, you can easily reach depths of 15 feet or more. In fact, some experienced flycasters fish weighted rabbit-fur flies much as you would fish jigs, working them over deep reefs and along deep weedlines.

Casting these large flies with a heavy fly rod (p. 49) can tire you out in a hurry, so it pays to concentrate on your prime spots and bypass marginal ones. Keep your retrieves short, only 10 feet or so, then cast again. This minimizes fatigue so you won't have to false cast as much.

POPULAR FLIES for pike and muskies include: (1) Whitlock's Hare Grub, a weighted rabbit-fur fly; (2) Seaducer, a streamer; (3) Umpqua Swimming Water Dog, a diver; and (4) Peck's Popper.

How to Construct a Fly Leader for Pike-Muskie Fishing

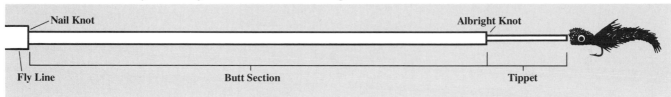

MAKE a leader using a butt section of 30- to 40-pound monofilament and a tippet of 15- to 40-pound nylon-coated braided wire. Use a 4- to 6-foot butt with a floating line, a 2- to 3-foot butt with a sinking line. In either case, the tippet should be about a foot long. Attach the leader butt to the fly line with a nail knot; to the wire with an Albright knot (see below). Twist-melt (p. 48) the fly to the tippet.

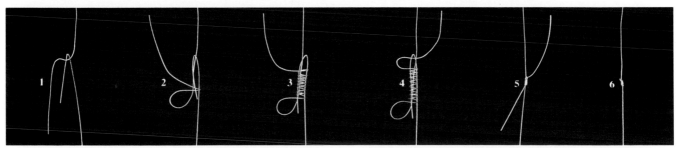

NAIL KNOT. (1) Lay a nail alongside the fly line and leader butt so 6 inches of the butt extends past the nail. (2) Begin wrapping the leader butt around the fly line, nail and standing portion of the leader. (3) Continue wrapping to make five loops. (4) Push the leader butt through the loops, following the gap made by the nail; remove nail. (5) Snug up the knot by pulling on the butt and standing portion of the leader. (6) Trim fly line and mono.

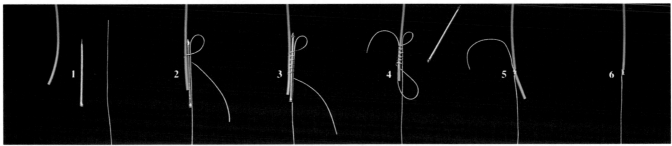

ALBRIGHT KNOT. (1) Double the end of a 16-inch length of twist-melt, then pass the mono through the opening. (2) Hold the mono against the twist-melt, then wrap the free end of the mono around the standing mono and twist-melt. (3) Make 8 wraps, progressing toward the opening. (4) Pass the free end of the mono back through the opening. (5) Tighten the knot by alternately pulling on the free end, then on the standing line. (6) Trim twist-melt and mono.

Fishing with Natural Bait

Whenever the water is cold or pike and muskies are "turned off," natural bait will likely outproduce artificial lures.

A good-sized pike or muskie will grab anything from an inch-long leech to a foot-long salamander, but bait-fishing devotees prefer baitfish, either live or dead, by a wide margin. Dead-bait fishing is most effective with oily baitfish such as smelt, ciscoes and shad. Evidently, their odor is stronger and more appealing.

Popular Pike & Musky Baits

Sucker

Shiner

Chub

Suckers are most popular for live-bait fishing, mainly because they're widely available. Some anglers prefer shiners or chubs, but pike or muskies seldom show a distinct preference. They're conditioned to strike any kind of fish they see.

The size of your baitfish, however, is crucial. Pike and muskies prefer larger bait than you might expect. For a 20-pounder, a 5-inch baitfish is barely a snack and probably not worth chasing. It takes one from $\frac{1}{4}$ to $\frac{1}{3}$ the length of the fish to generate much interest. A better choice for the 20-pounder, which measures at least 40 inches, would be a 10- to 14-inch baitfish. If you use small bait, you'll probably catch only small fish.

Keeping a dozen large baitfish alive is no easy task; they require a lot of oxygen, especially in warm weather. Even if you have an aerated live well or bait well in your boat, you'll need a good-sized aerated bucket or large Styrofoam cooler to get them from the bait shop to the water. Or, you can request an oxygen pack.

Wild baitfish are hardier, livelier and thus much more effective than those raised in a hatchery. If you can't find a bait shop that carries wild baitfish, you can seine, trap or catch them on hook and line in a nearby creek.

Bait fishermen tend to use hooks that are too small. The back or snout of a large baitfish fills up the hook gap so not enough of the point is exposed. The chart below shows the sizes of single, treble and quick-strike (p. 91) hooks you need. Attach your hook directly to a 20- to 30-pound braided-wire leader using a bowline or crimp (p. 49). Or, twist-melt it (p. 48) onto a nylon-coated leader.

One drawback to natural-bait fishing: pike and muskies often swallow the hook. Always carry a jaw spreader and needlenose pliers. If you plan to release a deeply hooked fish, cut the leader close to the hook rather than try to work the hook free.

Hook Size vs. Baitfish Size

BAITFISH SIZE	HOOK SIZE		
	Single	Treble	Quick-Strike
4-5 "	1/0, 2/0	4, 2	8
6-7 "	2/0-4/0	2, 1	6, 4
8-11 "	4/0-7/0	1, 1/0	4, 2
12-15 "	7/0-10/0	1/0-3/0	2-1/0

Smelt

Cisco

Waterdog

Still Fishing with Natural Bait

Still fishing works best when pike or muskies are concentrated in a precise spot or migrating through a confined area. Even a full-bellied fish will usually take a swipe at a lively minnow wiggling in its face. The two major still-fishing methods are bobber fishing and bottom fishing.

BOBBER FISHING. All anglers like to see their bobber plunge from sight, and nothing takes one down like a big pike or muskie. Although some regard bobber fishing as a technique for kids and old folks, there's no disputing its effectiveness.

Bobber fishing is a good way to catch pike or muskies in pockets in the weeds, along inside turns in the weedline, around cribs or in any high-percentage

spot. You can also drift a bobber rig over a weed flat or stump field, set it to a certain depth to fish a specific temperature layer or slowly troll it behind the boat to cover a lot of water.

The hardest part about bobber fishing is knowing when and how to set the hook. Some old-timers used to light a cigarette when their bobber went down. When they'd finished their smoke, they set the hook. But you don't have to wait that long if you pay attention to what the fish is doing. After taking the bait, it will normally make a short, fast run; stop to turn the bait; then slowly swim off again. Set the hook on the second run.

Selecting the right terminal tackle will also improve your hooking percentage. Don't make the mistake of using a bobber the size of a tennis ball, thinking that a big fish will have no trouble pulling it under. True,

FLOATS include: (1) slot-, (2) cylinder- and (3) tube-style slip-bobbers, for working deep water; (4) clip-on and (5) peg bobber, for fishing shallower water; and (6) pop-off bobber, rigged to detach from the line when a fish strikes (inset).

POPULAR RIGS for bobber fishing with live or dead baitfish include: (1) treble hook with one prong pushed through the back; and (2) quick-strike rig, with the leading quick-strike hook just ahead of the dorsal fin and the trailing hook near the pectoral fin. Another excellent rig for live baitfish is (3) a single hook pushed through the snout only. This rig is tied with a Sneck hook, which has a squared-off bend, so more of the hook point stays exposed.

a good-sized pike or muskie can easily swim off with a float that large, but the extra resistance increases the likelihood that it will drop the bait.

Use a bobber no larger than necessary to keep your rig afloat. Don't worry if the bait occasionally pulls the bobber down; there's no mistaking the tug of a minnow for the strike of a pike or muskie. A cylindrical float is a better choice than a round one. Because it rides higher, it's easier to see from a distance, yet there's less resistance when a fish pulls it under. You can eliminate resistance altogether by using a pop-off float (see above) that separates from the line when a fish bites.

In water less than 5 feet deep, a bobber secured to the line is adequate; in deeper water, a slip-bobber works better. You can fish deep, yet the float will slip to the end of the line for easy casting.

Another common mistake is using so much weight that the baitfish can barely move. When the fish aren't feeding aggressively, or when you're trying to keep your bait in a thin layer of cool water near the bottom, weight it down so it can't move much. Otherwise, let it swim freely. Add only a few split shot or a small sinker about 18 inches above the hook; if the weight is too close to the hook, the bait can't swim normally.

Most important is your choice of hook and method of hooking the bait. Veteran pike and muskie anglers continually debate the merits of a single hook versus a quick-strike rig.

For dead baits or live baits up to 12 inches long, it's tough to beat a quick-strike rig. The dual-hook arrangement helps hold a lifeless bait level and allows you to set the hook right away. It improves your hooking percentage with live bait, and because the fish don't have time to swallow it, they're seldom deeply hooked.

You can make a quick-strike rig using ordinary trebles, but many anglers prefer quick-strike hooks. The smaller barb is pushed into the bait, the larger one is exposed. On the hook set, the smaller hook tears out of the bait, making it easier to sink the larger hook into the fish.

Slide plastic shrink-tubing over the movable hook and heat with a lighter. You'll still be able to move the hook to adjust for the size of the bait, yet the hook won't slide freely on the leader.

Shrink-tubing keeps the movable hook from slipping too much

But with a large, lively baitfish, the rear hook of a quick-strike rig often tears out. A big single hook, from 3/0 to 12/0, works better. It lets the bait swim more freely and, if you're patient, will hook almost as many big fish, although you'll miss more small ones. One problem: if you let the fish swallow the bait, chances are they'll be deeply hooked. If you snip off the hook, however, the fish will probably survive.

BOTTOM FISHING. "Soaking" a live or dead baitfish on the bottom accounts for plenty of pike and muskies, especially in spring, when the fish are concentrated near their spawning areas. But this technique works in any situation where the bottom is relatively clean.

There's nothing complicated about bottom fishing. Just toss out your rig, prop up your rod, set your reel in free-spool with the clicker on and wait for a bite. Most anglers use the slip-sinker and quick-strike rigs shown below.

One drawback to bottom fishing: your bait tends to rest on the bottom where the fish won't see it, especially if the bottom is covered with even a thin layer of weeds or algae. A variety of rigs have been devised to keep the bait swimming higher, including the off-bottom rig shown below. To float a dead baitfish, stuff Styrofoam packing peanuts into its mouth, then hook it through the lips.

Popular Bottom-Fishing Rigs

QUICK-STRIKE RIG. Insert the trailing hook near the pectoral fin of a dead smelt or cisco, the leading hook between the dorsal fin and tail. This way, you can set the hook immediately when a fish grabs your bait.

OFF-BOTTOM RIG. A sinker holds this rig on the bottom, yet the bait is held well off bottom by a float and wire arm.

SLIP-SINKER RIG. Slide a slip sinker onto your line, then add a 3-foot braided-wire leader. Push a single hook or floating jighead through the baitfish's snout. This rig, also used for casting, trolling and drifting, allows a fish to take line without feeling resistance.

1. WATCH for any quick movements of your float. When a pike or muskie approaches, a lively baitfish will swim frantically, making the float dance.

2. FEED line when your float goes under. In most cases, a pike or muskie grabs the bait sideways and starts swimming away. If it feels resistance, it may drop the bait.

3. WAIT for the fish to stop, turn the bait and swallow it headfirst. Waiting time varies from 30 seconds to 30 minutes, depending on the size of the baitfish.

4. SET THE HOOK when the fish starts to move off. Make sure you reel up enough slack so you can feel the weight of the fish before setting.

Trolling, Casting and Drifting Natural Bait

These "do-somethin' " techniques are for anglers who quickly tire of sitting around waiting for a bobber to go under. They also make it possible to cover more water when you're searching for fish.

TROLLING. Old-time anglers had a simple technique for catching pike and muskies. They just tossed out a big sucker and slowly rowed along the shoreline. This method still works today, but thanks to modern electronics, your presentation can be much more precise. Instead of trolling randomly along shore, you can follow breaklines and work humps, greatly increasing your odds of encountering fish.

Old-timers used oars so they could move the bait very slowly. Don't try to troll with a big outboard motor; even the slowest speed would be much too fast, unless you were bucking a stiff wind. An electric trolling motor is ideal because you can precisely regulate your speed.

S-trolling almost always works better than trolling in a straight line. Swinging from side to side helps keep your lines away from the boat, so you're not as likely to spook fish, and allows you to cover more area. Also, the bait moves more erratically, speeding up and rising, then slowing down and sinking.

Depending on your trolling speed and the depth, you'll probably have to add a ⅜- to ¾-ounce sinker to get your bait deep enough. Some trollers add a bobber to their rig and motor along very slowly; that way, they can fish at exactly the level they want.

CASTING. With this technique, you can give your bait an erratic, darting action, much like that of a frightened or injured baitfish. By using a pumping retrieve with your rod pointed downward, you can impart a side-to-side motion similar to that of a jerkbait.

Another productive retrieve imitates a dying baitfish. Start with your rod level, sweep it sharply upward, then lower it back. The bait darts toward the surface, then sinks back again, just as a dying baitfish would do.

Suckers and chubs are the best choice for casting; they're tougher than shiners. Baitfish longer than 8 or 10 inches are difficult to cast, and you'll miss too many fish. A fresh dead bait that has not stiffened up is almost as effective as a live one.

When casting with suckers, there's no need to add sinkers, unless you're fishing in water more than 10 feet deep or the wind is pushing you along at a rapid clip. Even then, you'll need only a little weight, because suckers tend to swim down on their own. Chubs, however, may have to be weighted; they tend to swim toward the surface. To get your bait deeper, add a few split shot or poke them down the bait's gullet.

DRIFTING. This is a good way to cover large weed or gravel flats, or to work a distinct temperature layer. Weight your rig as you would for casting; hook on a live sucker, chub or shiner; let out enough line so your bait drifts just above the weeds or gravel or in the right temperature zone; set your rods in rod holders on the upwind side of the boat and let the breeze push you along.

You can control the path of your drift with an electric motor. If the wind pushes you too fast, throw out a sea anchor. When you reach the end of your drift, reel up your lines and motor back upwind, swinging wide to avoid motoring over the fish. Make another drift parallel to, but off to the side of, the first one.

The most widely used setup for casting, drifting or trolling is a simple slip-sinker rig (p. 92). But you should also be familiar with the rigs shown below.

Popular Rigs for Trolling, Casting and Drifting

WEEDLESS RIG. This is simply a slip-sinker rig with a single weedless hook and a bullet sinker. It allows you to pull baitfish through dense cover where an ordinary slip-sinker rig would quickly snag.

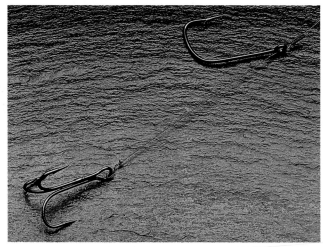

STINGER-HOOK RIG. Try this if fish are striking short. Haywire-twist (p. 48) single-strand wire to the eye of your main hook and a size 8 to 2 treble. Insert one point of the treble in the rear half of a baitfish or waterdog.

STRIP-ON SPINNER. This old standard is still one of the simplest and most effective rigs for dead baitfish. To rig a strip-on, push the wire shaft through the mouth and out

the rear, then slide the double hook though the eye of the wire shaft as shown (left). Pull on the wire to seat the hook with the points up (right).

LOB-CAST your bait with a smooth, sidearm motion. Otherwise, it will splash down too hard. You'll injure it or lose it after a few casts.

USE a hook with a molded-on weight to keep big baits on the bottom. This way, there is no sinker to snag in the rocks or pick up weeds.

DRIFT a live baitfish beneath the boat when casting with artificials, assuming multiple lines are legal. When a fish follows, try figure-eighting. Often, a fish that refuses the lure will grab the baitfish. Or, dangle one baitfish from the bow and another from the stern, then figure-eight between them.

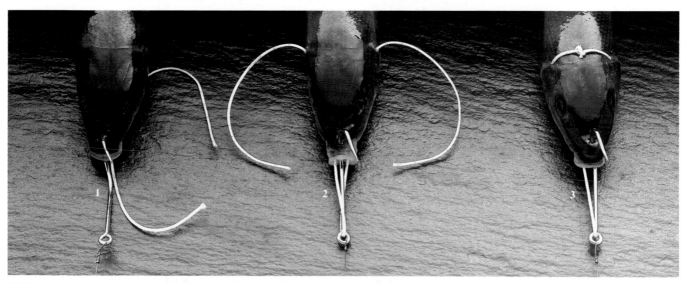

RIG your baitfish with a Dacron harness. This prevents the hook from tearing out, even after repeated casting. To make the rig, hook the baitfish through the snout, then (1) thread a 12-inch piece of braided-Dacron line through the mouth and out the gill. (2) Run the line through the hook eye, then thread it back through the mouth and out the other gill. (3) Tie the ends of the line on top of the head and trim any excess.

Techniques for Special Situations

LURES include: (1) spinnerbaits, such as Roland Martin Muskie Special, for all types of weeds; (2) buzzbaits, such as Blue Fox Double Buzzer, for weedtops; (3) brushguard jigs, such as Stanley Jig with Guido Bug trailer, for pockets and edges of all weeds; and (4) deep-running jerkbaits, such as Windel's Hunter, for deep weedlines.

Lures shown ⅓ actual size

Fishing Dense Weeds

Knowing what kinds of weeds to fish and when to fish them is perhaps the biggest challenge facing pike and muskie anglers. You've probably read that the fish prefer certain kinds of weeds and avoid other kinds. Unfortunately, it's not quite that simple.

Broad-leaved species of cabbage, for example, are widely considered to be the top pike and muskie producers. But that doesn't mean you'll automatically find fish when you find the right kind of cabbage.

A cabbage bed in a shallow bay, for instance, produces well in spring because the fish are still in the shallows after spawning and the water is cool enough for them to be comfortable. By summer, however, most of the larger fish have moved to deeper, cooler water, leaving only a few small stragglers. By fall, cool temperatures in the shallows kill the cabbage. Once it turns brown and the leaves start to deteriorate, it provides little cover and no longer produces oxygen, so the remaining fish move out.

The same kind of cabbage on a deep hump, on the other hand, holds no fish in spring. The water is too cold and the weeds are not fully developed. But as the cabbage grows lush in summer, it draws a lot of fish. Some remain into fall because the weeds do not turn brown as early as those in the shallows.

Ideally, pike-muskie weeds should have broad leaves to provide plenty of shade, they should be tall enough to give cover to fish cruising just beneath the surface, and they should be spaced widely enough to allow the fish to maneuver easily. However, if there are no weeds of this type growing in the areas the fish are using, they'll select some other type.

Emergent weeds, such as bulrushes, don't fit this description, but they draw plenty of pike and muskies in spring, when the fish are still in their spawning bays, and in fall, when submerged weeds start to die.

Floating-leaved weeds, such as lily pads, also hold pike and muskies in spring, and may continue to hold them in summer, assuming the beds do not become choked with other weeds. The dense overhead canopy keeps the water a few degrees cooler than surrounding water warmed by the sun.

Deep submergent weeds, such as coontail, attract pike and muskies from midsummer through fall. Often these weeds form a dense blanket several feet thick, so the fish cruise just above them or along the edges. Deep submergents remain green longer than other plants.

Different weed types dictate different lures and fishing methods. To fish emergents and floating-leaved weeds, use weedless lures, such as spinnerbaits, weedless spoons and brushguard jigs. For working the tops of submergent weeds, use topwaters, spinnerbaits and swimmer-head jigs. You can also fish weedtops with shallow-running crankbaits, minnow plugs, jerkbaits and bucktails; use deeper-running models to work deep weedlines. To fish a pocket, use a brushguard jig or weedless spoon, or helicopter a spinnerbait into it.

For tight pockets, toss out a minnow on a slip-bobber setup, or rig a minnow on a weedless hook and free-line it through the weeds. When the fish are scattered over large weed flats, try trolling with spinnerbaits.

Weed fishing requires heavier-than-normal line, not only to horse fish from heavy cover, but to reduce the chances that abrasion from stems and leaves will weaken the line. Use either braided Dacron or extra-tough mono. A longer-than-normal rod comes in handy for guiding your lure through the weeds (p. 104).

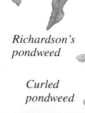

Good Weeds vs. Bad Weeds

CABBAGE. Broadleaf deep-water varieties, such as Richardson's pondweed (below left), make prime cover for pike and muskies, especially if the individual plants are loosely spaced. Narrowleaf shallow-water varieties, such as curled pondweed (below right), are seldom productive.

Richardson's pondweed

Curled pondweed

COONTAIL. Deep mats of coontail along a breakline (below) attract more fish than a thin layer on a flat bottom. Look for fish along the edges or top of the mat, or right in it under bright or cold-front conditions.

MILFOIL. Clumps of milfoil (below) or loosely spaced strands provide better pike-muskie cover and give the fish more room to move about than a thick, continuous milfoil bed.

Coontail

Milfoil

BULRUSHES. These emergents grow on a firm bottom in water as deep as 5 feet. Deep beds of hardstem or softstem bulrush with an irregular margin and many open pockets (below left) are best. Spikerushes (below right) grow only in shallow water and seldom hold good-sized pike or muskies.

Hardstem bulrush

Spikerush

WATERLILIES. Large pads, such as white or yellow waterlilies, with lots of openings and a distinct outside edge near deep water (below left), are better than small pads, such as water shield (below right), growing on a shallow flat.

White waterlily

Water shield

Tips for Fishing in Weeds

RUN the edges of a weedbed, looking for muskies cruising the shallows for food. If you spot one, come back a little later. Chances are it won't go far.

STEER your lure through slots and pockets in the weeds using a rod at least 7 feet long. A long rod also helps you control hooked fish.

STOP reeling when your weedless spoon or spinnerbait reaches a pocket in the weeds; keep your line taut as the lure slowly flutters down. Pike and muskies lying in the weeds will dart into the opening to grab the lure as it sinks, even though they're not actively feeding.

ATTACH your lure to a leader thin enough to cut through the weed stems when you retrieve.

SUBSTITUTE a weedless bass jighead for an open-hooked jighead. This way, you can fish right in the weeds.

CHECK weed types by running a deep-diving crankbait through them. Weeds will catch on the lip.

Speed Trolling

Trolling subsurface lures at speeds from 3 to 8 miles per hour is a deadly summertime technique for pike and muskies scattered over large weed flats or strung out along a weedline. You can cover the water in a hurry, and the fast-moving lures trigger lots of strikes.

With a short, stiff trolling rod and a level-wind reel spooled with 30- to 40-pound Dacron line, you should be able to keep your lure free of weeds. When the lure fouls, simply give your rod a sharp snap and the weeds will rip away.

Speed trolling with a hand-held rod will tire you out in minutes, particularly when using hard-pulling deep divers. Where legal, anglers use as many as 6 rods set in rod holders. This way, you can relax while covering a wider swath and varying your depths.

How to Speed-Troll a Weed Flat

LURES for speed trolling must run true at high speed. For shallow trolling, use: (1) bucktails, such as Peterson's Inhaler (this model has a small French blade); and (2) shallow-running crankbaits, such as a 6" Grandma.

LET OUT 40 to 80 feet of line and set your rods in upright rod holders to keep the lures running shallow. Steer the boat in a wide S-pattern to cover the weed flat and give the lures an erratic action.

How to Speed-Troll a Weedline

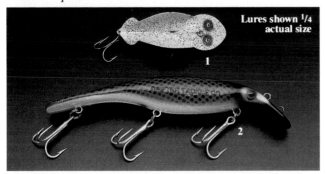

DEEP-TROLLING PLUGS include: (1) extra-deep runners, such as the Spoonplug; and (2) medium-deep runners, such as the Believer. For maximum depth, attach your leader to the Believer's rear eye.

RUN shorter lines, from 20 to 50 feet, when trolling along a weedline. Shorter lines give you better control so you can follow the weed edge more closely. To get your lures deep enough, set your rods in horizontal locking rod holders (p. 51).

Fishing Woody Cover

Standing timber, stumps, sunken logs, fallen trees and brush are important pike-muskie cover, particularly in rivers and man-made lakes, where water-level fluctuations may limit growth of aquatic plants.

In most cases, the best woody cover is adjacent to deep water. It protrudes well off bottom and has plenty of fine branches to attract baitfish. Newly flooded reservoirs have better woody cover than old ones; in time, the small branches rot away and the wood deteriorates.

Another important type of woody cover is the man-made fish attractor. Some of these devices are constructed much like a log cabin, with several layers of interlocking logs (opposite page). Others are merely piles of branches lashed together and weighted with cement blocks. Most often, these structures are placed in areas with little other cover.

To fish protruding treetops, brush piles, newly fallen trees or any other shallow woody cover that still has fine branches, use a spinnerbait, weedless spoon or topwater lure. Brushguard jigs, regular jigs with

Common Types of Woody Cover

ISOLATED CLUMPS of trees indicate an underwater hump, a prime pike-muskie hangout. Although the trees in this photo are apparent, older trees may have rotted off, leaving only submerged trunks or stumps.

TIMBERED POINTS that extend into the old river channel are good pike-muskie producers. The fish can feed in or along the edge of the timber, then easily retreat to deep water in the channel.

BRUSHY FLATS alongside a creek channel or the old river channel make excellent feeding areas for pike and muskies. You'll find most of the fish along the outside edge, where the flat drops into the channel.

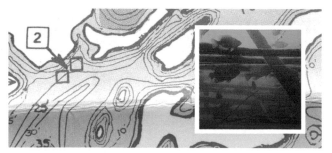

RESERVOIR MAPS often show exactly where fish attractors have been placed. The attractors (inset) draw panfish and other baitfish and, in turn, pike and muskies. On this map, the attractors are denoted with small squares.

light-wire hooks and crankbaits with the leading barbs of the trebles removed work well in deeper woody cover without many fine branches.

If you're convinced that a specific piece of woody cover is holding fish, but they're ignoring artificials, lower a quick-strike bobber rig (p. 91) with a live baitfish into or alongside the cover. When a fish bites, set the hook immediately and horse it out of the wood before it swims around a branch or log.

Sturdy tackle and heavier-than-normal line is a must when fishing the wood. Some reservoir anglers use line up to 50-pound test to pull fish out of the tangle. Heavy line also enables you to straighten hooks so you can free snagged lures. A lure retriever comes in handy too.

Suspended Pike & Muskies

Radio-tagging studies have proven that pike and muskies suspend more often than most anglers realize. This behavior is most common in deep, clear lakes and reservoirs with high populations of *pelagic* (open-water) baitfish. In some lakes, big muskies suspend after spawning, then move to shallow structure once the weeds develop.

Many anglers hesitate to fish for suspended pike and muskies; they believe their movements are random and discovering a pattern is impossible. But in most cases, the fish suspend near some type of structure or a school of baitfish, so locating them is not as much of a guessing game as you might think.

Trolling is the quickest way to find suspended fish. In natural lakes, motor along the edge of weedy shoreline

breaks, points and humps; in reservoirs, along the edge of old river or creek channels. Always S-troll, steering toward the structure, then away from it.

If you have no idea of the right depth, start trolling in the thermocline. Watch your depth finder closely for marks indicating fish or schools of baitfish, then set the depth of your lines accordingly. As a rule, pike hang a little deeper than muskies because they prefer cooler water.

When you're trolling through fish but can't trigger a strike, try motoring at double or even triple your normal speed. Or, try ripping the lure forward, then quickly dropping it back. The abrupt change of action often makes a difference.

You can get down as much as 30 feet with deep-diving crankbaits and minnow plugs, and another 5 to 10 feet with each ounce of lead added to your line. Trolling with downriggers (opposite page) or wire line will get you even deeper and give you more precise depth control. Refer to page 48 for recommendations on trolling rods, reels, line and leaders.

Downrigger Trolling for Pike and Muskies

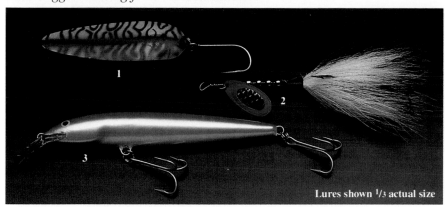

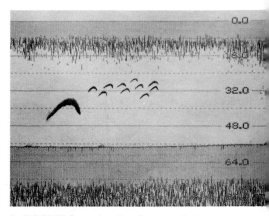

Lures shown 1/3 actual size

1. SELECT lures that don't dive too deep or pull too hard. Otherwise, you won't know how deep the lure is running, and you'll get too many false releases. Recommended lures include (1) spoons, such as the Eppinger Troll-Devle; (2) bucktails, such as Windel's Pike Harasser; and (3) shallow-running minnow plugs, such as the Floating Rapala Magnum.

2. SCOUT for schools of suspended baitfish with a good paper graph, video or liquid-crystal. The smaller marks on this tape are suspended ciscoes; the large mark, a pike.

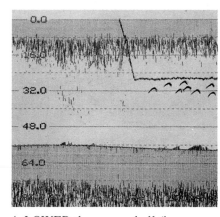

3. LET OUT about 10 feet of line and attach it to your release. Set the tension adjustment tight enough that the release doesn't trip from the pull of the lure.

4. LOWER the cannonball (heavy black line) so it tracks just above the baitfish. Pike and muskies are more likely to come up for a lure than go down for it.

5. SPEED UP when you get a strike. When your release trips, the line momentarily goes slack, giving the fish time to shake the hook. Speeding up reduces the chances that it will.

Tips for Catching Suspended Pike and Muskies

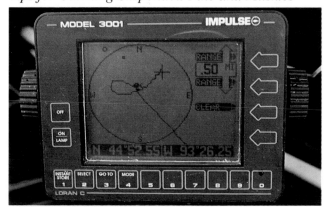

PINPOINT individual fish or baitfish schools with a Loran-C plotter. When you see something on your graph, enter its position (fish symbol) on the Loran. Continue trolling, turn around and troll through the same spot again.

TRY an occasional cast toward deep water when working a weedline. Or, have your partner cast out while you cast in. This way, you'll find out whether the fish are hugging the weeds or suspended over deep water.

Cold fronts may drive pike and muskies into dense weeds

Cold Fronts

Cold fronts top the list of excuses used by muskie anglers. It takes a severe cold front to slow the pike action, but even a mild cold front can shut down the muskies.

As a cold front approaches, the fish "turn on." They continue to feed heavily until the front passes. Then, the colder temperature, often coupled with clear skies and a strong northwest wind, causes the fish to move off the structure or bury themselves in weedy or woody cover. Feeding activity subsides as insect hatches stop and baitfish move out of the shallows.

The effects of a cold front are most noticeable on clear lakes, especially in spring when the fish are in shallow water. River fish are not immune to cold fronts, but show less response than lake fish.

You can increase your chances of catching cold-front pike and muskies by using the following tactics:

- Concentrate your efforts from late afternoon until just after dark, the time when the water temperature normally peaks. This may be the only time of day when the fish feed.

- Fish 5 to 10 feet deeper than normal. The ultra-clear skies allow sunlight to penetrate deeper.

- Stick with your prime spots, returning to them every couple of hours. Don't waste time exploring new water.

- Use live bait or smaller-than-normal lures and slow presentations.

- Present your lure or bait as close to the cover as possible. Cold-front fish are not chasers. A lure that bumps the cover may "wake them up."

- Try trolling just off structure where you've found fish before. This is the best way to catch fish that the cold front has pushed out of the weeds.

BEHAVIOR of pike and muskies changes dramatically with the passage of a cold front. Before the front, the fish (red) are moving about and feeding along the edges of a weedbed and on top of the weeds. But after the front passes, the fish (blue) are much less active. They bury in the weeds, suspend off to the side of them or move deeper.

Tips for Cold-Front Fishing

STILL-FISH high-percentage spots, such as pockets in the weeds, with a bobber rig. Even negative fish will move a few feet for a lively baitfish.

CAST a jig parallel to the weedline and retrieve it along the base of the weeds. This way, the jig stays close to fish tucked in the vegetation.

LOOK for narrows with current between two basins or between an island and shore. Fish in these areas continue to feed even under cold-front conditions.

Ultraclear Water

The sight-feeding habits of pike and muskies explain why they flourish in clear lakes – and why they're better able to scrutinize lures and spot sloppy presentations than are their murky-water relatives.

Deep, clear, oligotrophic lakes (p. 34) and early-stage mesotrophic lakes (p. 32) can be especially tough. Because the depths are well oxygenated, the fish have no trouble descending below the thermocline to pursue coldwater baitfish such as ciscoes. Instead of being tightly linked to cover, where they're easy to find, the fish spend much of their time suspended in open water (p. 108).

Clear-water fish are spookier too. They're more likely to spot your boat, see your shadow or notice a heavy line or leader.

But clear lakes produce some trophy-sized pike and muskies, so it pays to learn how to fish these waters. To improve your success, consider the following:

· Overcast, windy days are much better than sunny, calm ones.

· Pike and muskies tend to feed earlier and later in the day than in lower-clarity waters. Muskies may bite best at night.

· Try these lakes in spring and fall, when the fish are in the shallows, rather than in summer, when they're suspended.

· Select lures in natural colors, such as white, black, brown and gray. A small amount of fluorescent color, such as an orange spinner blade, may help, but the entire lure should not be fluorescent.

· Use lures that give you a little extra depth. Examples include deep-diving crankbaits, weighted jerkbaits and heavy bucktails. Small-diameter lines also get your lures a little deeper and are less likely to spook the fish.

· If you think you know where the fish are, but they won't bite, try live bait.

KEEP your distance when casting to pike or muskies in clear water; they're much spookier than their murky-water relatives. Wearing bright clothes or casting your shadow over the fish could also spook them.

Trolling with Planer Boards

Anglers who troll in ultraclear water share a common frustration: their boat spooks fish in shallow water, chasing them off to the side and away from the path of the lures. Trolling boards solve the problem by pulling the lines well to the side of the wake.

Another advantage: you can troll with multiple lines, covering a 100-foot-plus swath of water and increasing your odds of placing a lure near fish scattered over weed flats or suspended in open water. The technique and equipment is described below.

LET OUT the (1) planer boards using (2) reels attached to a 6-foot boom. Let out your outside (deepest) line and attach it to (3) a release. Pay out line and let the release slide down the cord, stopping it (4) just before the board. Set the (5) inside (shallowest) line the same way, then set the middle lines, stopping their releases (6 and 7) about halfway down each cord. The inside line may be only 20 feet long; the outside, 100 or more. Lures (from inside to outside) include: (8) propbaits, such as Poe's Awaker; (9) spinnerbaits, such as the Fudally Hawg Spin; (10) trolling plugs, such as the Cobb Bait; and (11) deep-diving crankbaits, such as the Phantom Diver.

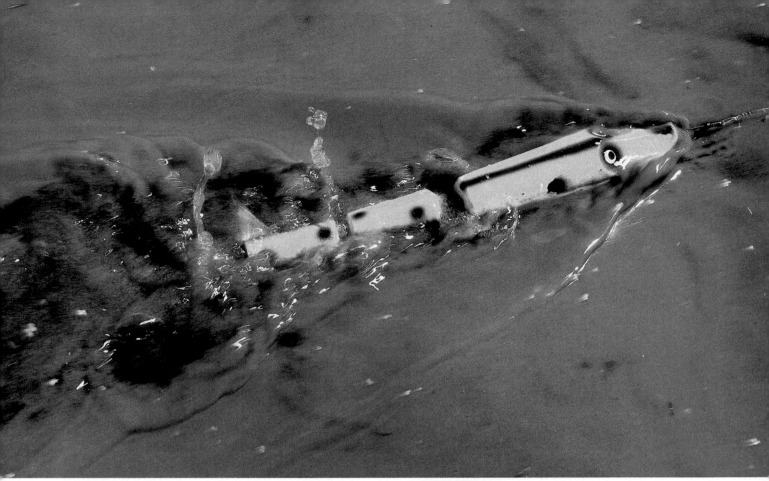

SELECT a topwater with an intense action when fishing low-clarity waters. Pike and muskies are most likely to notice lures that kick up a lot of water, and the commotion won't spook them.

Low-Clarity Waters

Pike and muskies thrive in some lakes where the visibility is only a few inches. They become accustomed to feeding in the discolored water, apparently using their lateral-line system (p. 12) more than vision.

Low clarity may be caused by an algae bloom, suspended silt or clay, or bog stain (opposite page). If the water is permanently discolored, the fish feed on a fairly regular schedule. But if the discoloration is temporary, usually the result of a heavy rain, vision feeders have trouble finding food – and anglers' lures. Fishing remains slow until the water starts to clear.

Most low-clarity lakes are shallow and eutrophic (p. 31). They warm sooner than most other lakes in spring and offer good early-season fishing. Normally, these lakes have little oxygen below the thermocline in summer, so the fish are confined to relatively shallow water. In fact, you'll commonly find them at depths of 15 feet or less all year, and sometimes in only a foot or two.

Panfish are the major food in many of these lakes, so pike and muskies spend much of their time cruising the weedy cover where the small fish live. But in ex-

tremely murky lakes, sunlight cannot penetrate deep enough to promote growth of rooted vegetation, so pike and muskies use other types of cover, such as rocks and logs.

Unlike clear lakes, where the fish usually bite best early and late in the day or at night, low-clarity lakes are better during the middle of the day. The "night bite" is apt to be slow. Calm, sunny weather generally shuts down the fishing in clear lakes, but not in murky ones.

Because the fish rely so heavily on their lateral-line sense to find food, large, noisy lures, including topwaters, rattling plugs and big-bladed spinnerbaits and bucktails, are excellent choices. Bright and fluorescent colors are usually more productive than drab ones.

Whatever lure you select, use a steady, rather than erratic, retrieve. This way, the fish can home in on the lure more easily. Always make a figure eight, or at least an L-turn, at the end of the retrieve, in case a fish is following.

Finesse is not much of an issue in these lakes. You don't have to worry about the fish seeing your boat or shadow, and you can get by with heavy lines and leaders. But don't go so heavy that your casting and lure presentation suffers.

Frequent Causes of Low-Clarity Water

BOG STAIN is caused by tannic acid, a by-product of decomposing plants. Although the water has a permanent coffee color, it is clearer than waters clouded by algae or silt.

ALGAE BLOOMS, especially those involving blue-green algae, give the water a pea-soup appearance. They're most common in highly fertile lakes during hot weather.

SILT OR CLAY particles are often kept in suspension by wave action or roughfish activity. Extremely fine clay particles form a permanent *colloidal suspension*.

Prime Pike-Muskie Locations in Low-Clarity Waters

SLOP, a mixture of lily pads and submerged vegetation, not only provides good cover, but also keeps the water beneath it slightly cooler than the surrounding water.

ROCKY POINTS or any exposed rock on the bottom holds pike and muskies, especially in lakes with little weedy or woody cover. It takes only a few big boulders to attract fish.

DOCKS make better pike-muskie spots in low-clarity waters than in clear ones. The fish are more likely to be in shallow water, and docks may be the best cover available there.

115

Dick Sternberg displays a trophy pike taken at the mouth of a tiny coldwater stream

Fishing Coldwater Pockets

" In the late '60s, Dick Sternberg, then a fisheries biologist on the Mississippi River, made a major pike-fishing breakthrough when he discovered that big pike were strongly drawn to spring holes and other coldwater pockets. Before that, everyone thought of pike as warmwater fish."

Ron Lindner – Publisher, In-Fisherman Magazine

The coldwater habits of big pike are now well known, and knowledgeable fishermen have long taken advantage of them by catching pike around various types of coldwater pockets in a body of warmer water (opposite page). Although anglers catch an occasional muskie around these spots, muskies are not attracted to the cold water nearly as much as pike.

When you catch a pike in a coldwater pocket, chances are it will be good sized, usually 7 pounds or larger. Smaller pike prefer warmer water and seldom inhabit these areas.

The coldwater habits of large pike were first documented in large river systems, but pike in natural and man-made lakes are no less drawn to cold water. In deep lakes, however, coldwater pockets may have less

TROUT STREAMS or other coldwater inlets flowing into a warmer river or lake will attract pike. If the stream is large enough, pike may swim upstream where they find cover in deep pools and around fallen trees.

UNDERWATER SPRINGS, similar to the surface springs shown above, often bubble up from the bottom in bays and harbors. The cold water forms small pockets that are difficult to find without a temperature gauge (p. 119).

SPRING SEEPS along shore are easy to find; shorelines in active spring areas often have dozens of them. Seeps are most likely to draw pike if there is deep water adjacent to the bank where they flow in.

drawing power because pike can find cold water simply by going below the thermocline, assuming the depths contain sufficient oxygen.

Coldwater pockets attract the most pike in summer, when the temperature difference between the pocket and the surrounding water is greatest. A differential of more than 30 degrees is possible; the pockets are often fed by groundwater of 50° F or less, while the surrounding water measures 80 or more. But it doesn't take a 30-degree temperature difference to draw pike; 7 or 8 degrees will do. The fish stay in the pockets until fall, when cooling water eliminates the temperature differential.

The best coldwater pockets are those that form in protected areas (photo at right). Otherwise, even a big spring has little drawing power.

COLDWATER STREAMS that enter along open shorelines (right) or flow into moving water are less likely to draw pike than streams flowing into bays, backwaters or other protected areas (left). There, the cold water stays put rather than being mixed by the wind or carried away by the current.

117

Another consideration is the wind. In calm weather, even a trickle of cold water can form a pocket large enough to attract pike. But a strong wind mixes the water completely, eliminating any small coldwater pockets on the bottom and dispersing the pike.

The wind also affects summertime pike location in large lakes, even if there are no springs or coldwater inlets. An offshore wind cools the water along shore, an onshore wind warms it (opposite page).

Coldwater pockets at least 5 feet deep are the most consistent producers, although shallower pockets may also hold pike. Sometimes the fish swim far into a shallow bay to reach a spring hole in water only one or two feet deep.

But coldwater pockets in shallow water may not hold fish throughout the day. Under a strong midday sun, pike sometimes retreat to deeper water.

You can find coldwater pockets by searching with a temperature gauge in summer, but it's much easier to look for them after freeze-up. If you see an area of open water along shore, it's probably a spring. Groundwater maintains the same temperature year-round, so it's colder than the surrounding water in summer, but considerably warmer in winter.

How to Fish Different Kinds of Spring Holes

DEEP SPRING HOLE. Underwater springs come in from the bottom, creating a distinct layer of cold water (blue) that hugs the bottom because it's heavier than the warm water. You must keep your bait in this layer, and slip-bobber fishing is one sure way to do it. Jigs also work well, as do deep-running crankbaits and minnow plugs.

SHALLOW SPRING HOLE. Springs flowing in from shore draw pike into very shallow water. Cast a topwater such as a buzzbait or propbait right into the spot where the cold water enters. Other good choices are bucktails, spinnerbaits, shallow-running plugs and an unweighted baitfish beneath a float.

Tips for Locating Coldwater Sources

CHECK the water temperature with a battery-operated temperature gauge. This way, you can quickly locate the outer edges of the coldwater zone and determine the thickness of the layer.

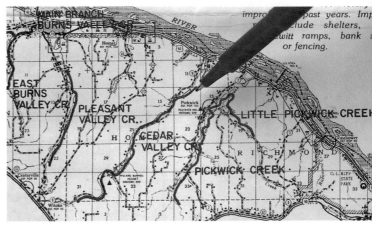

DETERMINE where trout streams flow into warmwater lakes and streams by referring to a trout-stream guide. These free publications are available from many state natural-resources agencies.

SCOUT for open water along icebound shorelines. The water may be open because of inflowing springs, which are considerably warmer in winter than the river or lake water. Return to fish these areas in summer.

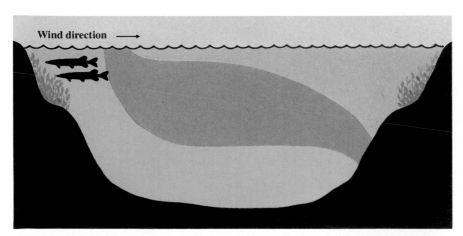

Wind direction →

WAIT for an offshore wind to catch summertime pike in stratified lakes. An offshore wind pushes warm water away from shore, and cooler water from the depths wells up to replace it. The water temperature along shore may drop several degrees, enough to draw pike into weedbeds and other cover along shore where the water had previously been too warm.

LOOK for spring holes in boat harbors, especially those that have been dredged. The dredging often opens springs, and the cold water can collect in an area sheltered on all sides from the wind.

Night Fishing

WEAR a headlamp covered with green cellophane when night fishing. The light enables you to see most follows, yet it won't spook the fish. Another trick: draw your lure through the area illuminated by your green bow light.

Until recently, night fishing for Esocids was thought to be a waste of time; anglers believed the fish fed only in daylight hours. This is usually a safe assumption in regard to pike, but night fishing for muskies produces some impressive catches, especially on clear lakes or lakes with heavy daytime boat traffic. Hybrids have an intermediate tendency to bite after dark.

Night-fishing action peaks in midsummer, when the surface temperature is warmest. Night stalkers prefer hot, calm, muggy weather, along with a full moon. Night fishing after a cold front is not as productive, although muskies may bite for an hour or so after dark.

At night, you'll find muskies on the same structure as in daylight hours, but much shallower. It's not unusual to catch them in water less than 2 feet deep.

Following a calm day with steadily rising temperatures, try topwater baits or bucktails; on a windy night or after a day of falling temperatures, try a crankbait or other subsurface lure. The fish aren't likely to notice a topwater when the surface is choppy.

Select lures that can be retrieved slowly and steadily, yet make a lot of noise or produce strong vibrations. If you use a lure with an erratic action, fish won't be able to home in on it and they'll often miss it. Many anglers prefer black lures, but color is less important than size; larger lures make larger silhouettes.

Be sure to set out markers in daylight so you can easily find your spots after dark. Carry a strong spotlight so you can see the markers from a distance. If you motor over the fish in an attempt to find your spot, they'll move away.

Some anglers make the mistake of setting a lantern in their boat in an attempt to see better. Although a bright light illuminates the area around the boat, it impairs distance vision, so you won't be able to see casting targets or surface strikes. With no light, your eyes will adjust to the darkness in 15 minutes or so.

When you see or hear a fish "blow up" on your lure, resist the urge to set the hook. Sometimes, they'll slash at it 3 or 4 times before they get it. Don't set the hook until you feel the weight of the fish.

It pays to keep your boat orderly when fishing at night. Close your tackle box and stash any excess gear to prevent unnecessary tangles. Always carry an extra rod in case of a bad snarl or backlash.

Lures shown ¹/₂ actual size

POPULAR LURES include: (1) bulky, large-bladed spinnerbaits, such as the M-G Spinnerbait; (2) good-sized crankbaits, such as the Phantom Diver; and (3) noisy topwaters, such as Mouldy's Topper Stopper.

Night-Fishing Tips

ATTACH a strip of luminescent tape to the top of your lure, then illuminate it with a strong flashlight or camera strobe. The glowing tape helps you see the lure, so you won't wind it in too far and ruin your tip top.

CLAMP a shop light to the gunwale after replacing the bulb with a 60-watt, 12-volt RV bulb. Turn the light on only when you want to land a fish. Otherwise, it may spook any fish following your lure.

MAKE a lighted marker (left) by inserting a cyalume light stick inside a milk jug. Tie an 8- to 12-ounce weight to the neck so the jug rides upright; attach a cord and anchor to the handle. Set markers on each spot you want to fish

(right). Shut off your engine and use an electric motor to approach your spot, staying far enough away that you can just reach it with a long cast. This way, you won't spook the fish and they'll have more time to home in on the lure.

EXTREMELY LOW WATER in reservoirs, usually the result of fall drawdowns, drives pike and muskies out of shallow portions of the main lake and the creek arms and into the old river channel and deep creek channels.

Fluctuating Water

The challenge in fishing pike or muskies in rivers and reservoirs is knowing where to find them and how to fish them at different water stages. Any change in water level, current speed or water clarity generally upsets the normal pattern.

After a heavy rain, for example, a river may rise several feet overnight, and the normally clear water looks more like heavily creamed coffee. The fast current forces most of the fish out of their usual haunts and into newly created eddies along the bank. If the rising water spills over the bank into adjacent lowlands, the fish will move into the flooded area to escape the current.

The muddy water requires lures that are highly visible and produce a lot of noise or vibration. Good choices include bulky bucktails and spinnerbaits with large Colorado blades, big rattling plugs and noisy topwaters.

As a rule, the fish continue to feed as long as the water is rising. One theory is that the rising water washes in food for smaller fish, activating them and, in turn, stimulating pursuit by predators. Feeding usually slows when the water starts to drop and the fish move to deeper structure.

Water-level changes need not be severe to cause problems for anglers. Often, a rise or drop of only a few inches displaces the fish, and an even smaller drop may slow the bite. As a rule, the faster the water drops, the poorer the fishing.

In big rivers, falling water forces pike and muskies out of shallow backwaters and into the main channel. In smaller rivers, the fish move into the deepest pools. Fish confined in pools are extremely vulnerable. As their food supply dwindles, they grow hungrier and thus easier to catch.

In reservoirs, rising water brings the fish closer to shore and farther back into the creek arms. You'll find them on shallow, timbered flats, along the bases of rocky bluffs and way up into secondary and tertiary creek arms. When the water drops, they move back to the river or creek channels.

River and reservoir anglers pay close attention to water-level gauges, noting not only the reading at the moment, but also whether the water is rising or falling. Along many big rivers, you can get water-level and flow information from local Army Corps of Engineers offices.

Where to Fish Rivers in High Water

FLOODED TREES. The best ones are large enough to create a good-sized eddy on the downstream side.

FLOODED BRUSH. Look for large clumps along the shoreline or on shallow flats.

SLACK-WATER POCKETS. Fish hold in these spots as long as the water is rising or stable.

Where to Fish Rivers in Low Water

WEED BEDS. The fish are most likely to hold in beds of green weeds, especially broad-leaved cabbage, in the main channel or in side channels with light current.

POOLS BELOW RAPIDS. These spots draw a wide variety of baitfish and gamefish in low water, so they make ideal pike-muskie feeding areas.

Tips for Monitoring Water Levels

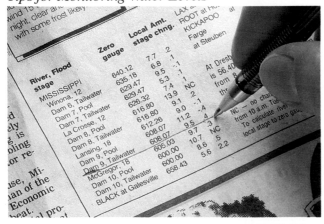

CHECK local newspapers for present water stage, daily change and volume of flow. Newspapers in most good-sized cities near major rivers or reservoirs publish this information daily.

KEEP a logbook that shows where you caught fish at different water levels, and whether the water was rising, falling or stable. Then, return to those spots in the future, when water conditions are the same.

Ice Fishing

Even before ice forms on lakes and river backwaters, pike go on a feeding binge that continues for several weeks after freeze-up. Some of the year's fastest action takes place during this period.

Pike feed more actively than most other gamefish in winter. Muskies feed very little once the water temperature falls below 40 degrees, but ice fishermen occasionally catch one by accident.

WHERE TO FIND PIKE. In early winter, look for them in shallow, weedy bays, especially around large patches of green weeds. Before freeze-up, try to locate weedy areas likely to produce once the ice forms. You can also find green weeds by peering down holes in the thin ice.

By midwinter, most pike have moved out of the bays into deeper water, although small pike sometimes stay in the bays all winter. Larger pike may stay around too, if the bay has deep enough water. Weedy cover becomes less important in midwinter; most pike hold along the edges of deep points, humps or rock piles.

Pike activity slows in midwinter, but they may be more concentrated. If you find the right spot, you'll catch plenty of fish. If your lake is prone to oxygen sags in winter, you'll probably find the pike right under the ice, where the oxygen level is highest. Pike return to the shallow bays in late winter and feed heavily until ice-out.

River pike spend most of the winter in weedy bays and backwaters. They remain in these slackwater areas as long as the oxygen level holds up. Once it starts to sag, however, they move closer to the current, often to the mouth of the bay or backwater or into the main river. When the ice begins to thaw in late winter, pike return to their early winter spots.

TIP-UP FISHING. Tip-ups account for the vast majority of pike taken through the ice. Where it's legal to fish with more than one line, groups of fishermen commonly set out a spread of tip-ups large enough to cover an entire bay or sunken island. While watching their tip-ups, anglers often jig with another line.

The term *tip-up* means a device with a spring-loaded flag that stands upright when you get a bite. Most tip-ups are designed to prevent the line from freezing into the hole. They have underwater reels so the line won't freeze on the spool.

Tip-up fishermen generally use live baitfish from 5 inches to more than a foot long, but dead smelt and ciscoes are gaining in popularity. Some anglers feel that dead bait works better when pike are inactive and don't want to chase a lively minnow.

Spool tip-ups with 25- to 40-pound Dacron line or nylon-coated tip-up line. The latter doesn't soak up water, so it won't freeze on above-water reels. Rig baitfish as you would for bobber fishing (p. 91), using a 20- to 30-pound braided-wire leader and a single hook, treble hook or quick-strike rig. A Swedish hook (p. 127) also works well for dead baitfish.

Common Types of Tip-Ups

SPINDLE tip-ups are the most popular and reliable type. They have a (1) plastic or wooden frame that rests on the ice and (2) an underwater reel. When a fish bites, the reel turns an internal shaft attached to a (3) spindle, tripping the (4) flag. You can increase the trip tension to prevent a large baitfish from springing the flag by setting the flag arm in the slot on the spindle (inset).

WIND tip-ups give the bait action, but with the (1) arm above water, the line may freeze in. Wind blowing on the (2) metal plate moves the arm. A bite turns the (3) reel and trips the (4) flag.

MAGNETIC tip-ups (left) can be adjusted so the trip tension is very precise. When the tip-up is set (cutaway at right), a (1) magnet on the (2) reel pulls on (3) another magnet on the (4) spring-loaded flag shaft, preventing the reel from turning and holding the flag down. When a fish bites, the reel turns, breaking the magnetic tension and allowing the flag to pop up. You can adjust the trip tension simply by loosening a (5) setscrew and moving the spool up or down.

ECONOMY tip-ups also have an underwater reel that trips a flag when a fish bites, but the trip tension cannot be adjusted. Consequently, there's no way to prevent a big, lively baitfish from springing the flag.

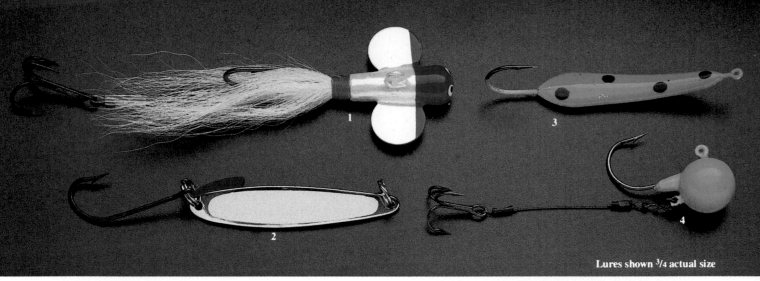

Lures shown ³/₄ actual size

POPULAR JIGGING LURES include: (1) airplane jigs, such as the Northland Airplane Jig in ½- to 1½-ounce sizes; (2) jigging spoons, such as the Swedish Pimple in sizes 5 to 7 with a single hook instead of a treble and (3) ³/₈-ounce Jig-A-Whopper Walleye Hawger; and (4) ¼- to ³/₈-ounce lead-head jigs, such as the Northland Fireball with removable stinger hook. Tip all of these lures with a 3- to 4-inch minnow.

JIGGING. Although jigging has not gained widespread popularity, it offers some definite advantages over tip-up fishing. Because you can move around more easily, you can keep trying new holes until you find the fish. And the jigging action will sometimes trigger strikes from pike that refuse a stationary bait.

Select a fairly stiff jigging rod about 3½ feet long and a spinning or baitcasting reel with 8- to 12-pound mono. Whatever reel you select, make sure it has a smooth drag that works well in subfreezing weather. If you have a spinning reel with a sticky drag, just leave the antireverse lever off and backreel.

Any good-sized jigging lure will catch pike. Flashy or bright colors such as silver, red-and-white and chartreuse generally work best. When the fish are aggressive, try large lures; when they're finicky, use smaller ones. You can also jig with a dead baitfish on a quick-strike rig.

An interesting technique developed by guides in northern Wisconsin is jigging with strips of meat from whatever kind of baitfish the pike normally eat. Impale several fresh 3- to 6-inch strips on a treble hook and jig it up and down to produce an enticing wiggle. The action combined with the natural smell often has more appeal than bait-shop minnows.

OTHER TECHNIQUES. Besides tip-ups, pike fishermen use a wide array of clever devices, some store-bought and some handmade, to signal bites. Probably the oldest, but still one of the best, is a simple willow stick embedded in a pile of slush so the tip extends directly over the hole. The line drapes over the end of the stick, and when a fish bites, the willow bends until the line slips off. The willow is flexible enough that you can see the action of the minnow. When a pike approaches, the minnow gets excited and starts swimming violently, bobbing the willow and alerting you to the possibility of a strike.

Some anglers claim that a willow works even better than a tip-up because it persuades pike to take the bait. If the bait feels lifeless, a pike may drop it. But a springy willow makes it feel like the bait is pulling back, so the pike is more likely to swallow it.

Another effective method: freeze the handle of an ordinary baitcasting outfit into the slush. Put the clicker on for a little tension and attach a bobber or cloth flag as a strike indicator. When a fish bites, the rod enables you to set the hook much harder and fight the fish more easily than you could with a tip-up.

ACCESSORIES. Before drilling any holes, use a portable flasher to check the depth and look for weeds (opposite page). If there's not too much snow or slush, you can pour a little water on the ice, place your transducer in it and take a reading.

Once you find the right area, drill plenty of holes so you can move around. A power auger makes the job easy. The blade should be at least 9 inches in diameter. It's tough to lead a good-sized pike into a small hole in the ice, and a trophy-sized fish could wedge into the hole. Be sure to carry an extra set of auger blades because they dull easily.

You may want to widen the bottoms of your holes with an ice chisel; this way, you can easily lead the fish into the hole. A chisel also works well for testing ice thickness.

Other useful equipment includes an ice scoop for clearing your holes, a hand towel, a gaff, a thick-walled Styrofoam bucket to hold large minnows and prevent the water from freezing, and a minnow net.

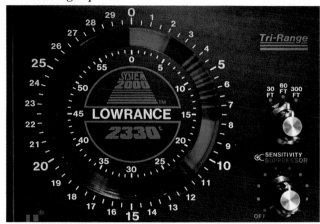

SCOUT with your depth finder to find any remaining clumps of green weeds. Pour a little water on the ice and place your transducer in the puddle; it will shoot through clear ice and show weeds just as well as in summer.

GRAB a pike behind the head as it comes through the hole and toss it off to the side. Otherwise, it could flop back down the hole. Don't try this with big pike, however. Their backs are too wide for you to get a good grip.

GAFF pike only if you intend to keep them. You can safely release a pike if you gaff it through the mouth as shown above, but if you gaff it in the body or injure its gills, it probably won't survive.

PREVENT your tip-up line from unwinding when not in use by wrapping the line around the reel handle (inset), then attaching the hook to a thick rubber band wrapped around the opposite end of the tip-up frame.

USE a Swedish hook (size 3 or 4) for rigging dead baitfish. With the hook shank down, push the hook into the vent as far as the bend, then turn the shank up and push the hook point through the back just behind the head.

Trophy Fishing

"...fifty years on the water has taught me conclusively that the really big muskies are in deep water..."

Len Hartman – holder of 5 world line-class muskie records

What Hartman observed about muskies also holds for northern pike and for many other fish species. As they grow larger they prefer cooler water, which usually means they'll be found deeper than the smaller members of their breed. This deepwater pattern is strongest in summer. At other times of the year, the fish can find cool enough water in the shallows.

Hartman discovered that he could catch larger muskies by trolling than by casting, mainly because trolling allowed him to keep his lure in deep water more of the time.

Because large northern pike have a stronger penchant for cold water than do muskies, they're often found at even greater depths in summer, assuming there is adequate food

Len Hartman displays a 65-pound muskie caught by deep-trolling in New York's St. Lawrence River

and oxygen. Pike also satisfy their need for cold water by congregating in spring holes (p. 117).

Until recently, most writers have linked pike and muskies to shallow, weedy water. Paintings often show the fish lurking in dense weeds or rocketing skyward out of a thick weedbed. The scarcity of big pike in summer is usually attributed to sore mouths resulting from the loss of teeth. In reality, however, pike and muskies in most waters feed heavily in summer. They just don't spend much time in the places most anglers expect to find them.

Fishing the shallows makes sense in spring and fall, when the water is cool, although the fish may go deep in late fall. But in summer, the odds are with the angler who works deeper water.

Not to say that you'll never catch a big pike or muskie in the shallows in summer, but in most waters, it's an oddity. Muskie anglers who ply shallow weedbeds catch a few respectable fish, but most admit that the going gets tough when warm weather sets in.

Shallow weedbeds that do attract big pike and muskies in summer have one thing in common: deep water nearby. Evidently the fish rest in the depths, then move into the weeds to feed. Seldom will you find trophy-caliber pike or muskies in a shallow weedbed far from deep water.

Just how deep is deep? It all depends on the type of water. In a shallow, eutrophic lake, for instance, the depths lack oxygen in summer, so the fish can't go below the thermocline. If there is adequate oxygen, however, the thermocline is no barrier. In Ontario's gigantic Lake Nipigon, for example, pike have been netted in water more than 100 feet deep.

When the fish go deep, locating them can be a problem. Some relate to deep humps or points; others roam open water, if that's where the food is. In deep, oligotrophic lakes, for example, trophy-sized pike and muskies feed heavily on ciscoes and whitefish, both of which often suspend over deep water.

Anglers equipped with good electronics can graph the fish, then troll for them using lead-core or wire line, or downriggers.

Some deep-diving crankbaits can reach depths of 30 feet or more if you use small-diameter mono from 12- to 20-pound test. But fish suspended in open water are rarely enthusiastic biters. And the spot where you catch them one day may not produce the next.

Muskies on shallow structure don't roam as much as those in open water. Should a big muskie follow your lure, but refuse to strike, note the location; the fish will probably stay in the general vicinity. Trophy hunters sometimes work on the same muskie for months before they finally catch it. Big pike are much less likely to hang out in a specific area.

Most trophy specialists recommend big lures for catching big fish, but there are times when you'll do better on smaller lures. In lakes where small perch are the main forage, for instance, a 6-inch lure may be more effective than a 12-incher. Smaller-than-normal lures also work better in early

spring, after a cold front or at other times when the fish are not feeding actively.

Many trophy hunters swear by huge live baitfish, usually suckers from 14 to 20 inches long. But baitfish this large are hard to find, so you'll probably have to catch your own (p. 131).

With these big baits, you may have to wait 10 minutes or more to set the hook. If you follow the recommended procedure of letting the fish swim off, stop to swallow the bait and then swim off again before you set, chances are the fish will be deeply hooked.

If you want to release your fish, pinch down or file off the barb before you start fishing. The chart below will help you estimate the weight if you know the length and girth.

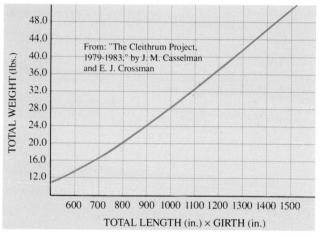

ESTIMATE the weight of fish you release using the above graph. The curve was computed for muskies, but it works equally well for pike. Measure the length of the fish (from the tip of the snout to the tip of the tail) and multiply by the girth (greatest measurement). Find this number at the bottom, follow straight up to the curve, then follow across to find the weight.

This 15-inch sucker (shown actual size) is just right for trophy pike and muskies

Quick-strike rigs can reduce hooking mortality, but they don't work well with extremely large baitfish because the hooks often tear out. The quick-strike rig shown on the opposite page, however, will solve the problem. You'll be able to set the hook right away and greatly reduce deep-hooking losses.

As a rule, your best chances for big fish are in big waters – large lakes and river systems. Just as goldfish attain only a small fraction of their size potential in an aquarium, pike and muskies seldom reach maximum size in small lakes or streams. And even if they did, the odds of their succumbing to a well-placed lure are considerably higher.

One notable exception to the big water/big fish rule: even small lakes with a good supply of salmonid (salmon family) forage often produce gigantic pike and sometimes muskies. Western trout lakes with good populations of kokanee salmon, for instance, yield astounding numbers of 20- to 30-pound pike because of the coldwater, high-fat food. Some of these lakes are only a few hundred acres in size.

Of course, the best way to boost your chances of connecting with a trophy is to fish in waters that have a lot of them. Refer to "Prime Pike and Muskie Waters" (pp. 134-155) for information on trophy hot spots throughout the United States and Canada.

The chart below shows the relative trophy potential of each important type of pike and muskie water. It also lists the time of year when the biggest fish are usually caught.

Where and When to Catch Trophy Pike and Muskies

LAKE TYPE	TROPHY POTENTIAL		PEAK TIMES	
	PIKE	MUSKIE	PIKE	MUSKIE
Eutrophic	*Poor*. Yields occasional trophies if there is a source of cool water.	*Poor-Fair*. Lightly fished lakes occasionally produce a real trophy.	*Fall to Early Winter*. As the water cools and the baitfish crop thins, pike spend more time feeding.	*Spring, Fall*. Wait until the algae die-off in early fall clears the water.
Mesotrophic	*Fair-Good*. The best ones have adequate oxygen below the thermocline all summer.	*Good-Excellent*. Deep lakes with high-fat forage, such as ciscoes, are best.	*Late Fall to Early Winter*. These lakes cool later than eutrophic lakes, so the fall bite is later.	*Late Summer thru Fall*. Cool water concentrates fish in weedbeds, where they're easy to find.
Oligotrophic	*Good-Excellent*. Look for lakes that haven't been discovered by the masses.	*Good-Excellent*. Don't waste your time on the "numbers" lakes.	*Early Spring, Late Fall*. Fishing peaks when the water drops to 45° and ciscoes move in to spawn.	*Late Summer, Late Fall*. The late-fall cisco pattern produces the biggest fish, as it does for pike.
Shallow Reservoir	*Poor-Fair*. Fairly new reservoirs with booming baitfish populations are better than old reservoirs.	*Fair-Good*. Larger, deeper reservoirs are better bets for a trophy; the fish are less vulnerable to angling.	*Fall*. Cooling water draws baitfish onto shallow flats; pike follow.	Spring, Fall. Like eutrophic lakes, shallow reservoirs turn on early in spring and fall.
Mid-Depth Reservoir	*Fair-Good*. The best ones have many deep channels where the fish can go when the water warms or drops.	*Fair-Good*. Lakes with large shad crops produce the most big fish.	*Early Spring, Fall*. Look for pre-spawn pike in the back ends of shallow creek arms.	*Fall*. The fish concentrate on shallow structure adjacent to deep water.
Mid-Size River	*Poor-Fair*. The lower reaches, where the river is widest and deepest, yield the biggest pike.	*Poor-Fair*. Those with large, deep pools have the best trophy potential.	*Early Spring, Fall*. The fish concentrate in deep pools when the river is low in fall.	*Late Summer thru Fall*. Tailwaters and deep pools almost always hold fish; they bite best in low water.
Big River	*Good-Excellent*. Rivers far enough north to have cool water or those with lots of coldwater pockets (p. 117) produce the most trophies.	*Good-Excellent*. The best big rivers have relatively clear water and a rock-gravel-sand, rather than silt, bottom.	*Early Spring, Summer*. Look for pre-spawn fish in shallow sloughs; summer-time fish on weed flats or in coldwater pockets.	*Fall*. Look for muskies around deep sand or gravel bars in the main channel.

Tips for Catching and Using Big Baitfish

CATCH big suckers, redhorse or chubs in a small stream. Using a light spinning outfit and a rig consisting of a split-shot, size 6 hook and a worm, cast into a riffle and drift the bait into a pool. Keep a few of the baitfish in a cooler or large, aerated bait bucket .

MAKE a pop-off slip-bobber rig using a 2½- to 3-inch Styrofoam ball. Poke a hole in the ball with a pencil; insert a peg rigged as shown so the line can slip. Add a 1-ounce sinker to hold down the bait; an 18-inch, 40-pound, braided-wire leader; and a size 8/0 to 12/0 Sneck hook.

PREVENT a big baitfish from getting off the hook by using a "keeper" made from a piece of heavy rubber band or surgical tubing. Push one end of the keeper onto the shank, hook the baitfish through the snout, then push the other end of the keeper over the hook point as shown.

DRIFT a bobber rig through the area you want to fish; continual casting will soon kill the baitfish. Let the rig out behind the boat and allow the wind to push you along slowly, using your electric trolling motor to control your drift path and speed.

How to Make a Quick-Strike Rig for Large Baitfish

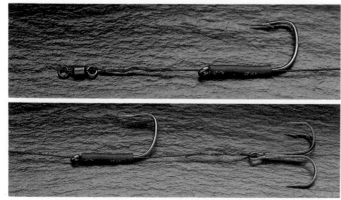

TWIST-MELT (p. 48) a barrel swivel onto a 2-foot section of plastic-coated, 40-pound leader. Slip on a ¾-inch piece of shrink-tubing and a size 8/0 to 12/0 Sneck hook; heat the tubing to shrink it onto the hook shank (top left). Twist-melt a size 2/0 to 4/0 treble hook to the other end of the leader and bend two of the hooks so they're about ½ inch apart (bottom left). Push the single hook through the snout and two hooks of the treble into the back, just behind the dorsal fin (right). Pull the leader through the shrink-tubing to snug it up.

Prime Pike & Muskie Waters

States with prime pike and muskie waters

MAINE

VT.

N. H.

NEW YORK

MASS.

R. I.

PENNSYLVANIA

CONN.

N. J.

MD.

W. VIRGINIA

DEL.

VIRGINIA

The East

In years past, the eastern region was famed for its trophy pike and muskie fishing. In 1940, New York's Sacandaga Reservoir gave up a 46-pound, 2-ounce pike that held the world record for more than 50 years and still stands as the North American record. In the 1950s and 60s, the St. Lawrence River in upper New York was the continent's undisputed muskie hot spot, producing dozens of fish in the 50- to 60-pound class, including a 69-pound, 15-ouncer caught in 1957. This fish still holds the world record.

But in those days, fishing pressure was not much of a factor; today, it is. In many eastern waters, particularly those near metropolitan areas, pike and muskies face an unrelenting barrage of lures and baits. On a weekend, it's not unusual to see 100 boats on a 200-acre lake. With pressure this heavy, good-sized fish are hard to come by.

Pike and muskies are found throughout the region, with the exception of Delaware, New Hampshire and most of Maine. The fish inhabit almost every possible type of water, from huge natural lakes to water-supply reservoirs to small streams. Because of the intense fishing pressure, most pike and muskie populations must be bolstered by stocking. Many of these states, in an attempt to provide bigger fish in more waters, are stocking tiger muskies instead of pike.

For quality pike or muskie fishing, concentrate on the large lakes or big river systems, where the fish are better able to elude anglers. For instance, Lake Champlain, a 280,000-acre meso lake in New York and Vermont, yields good numbers of 10- to 15-pound pike. In Pennsylvania's 14,650-acre Pymatuning

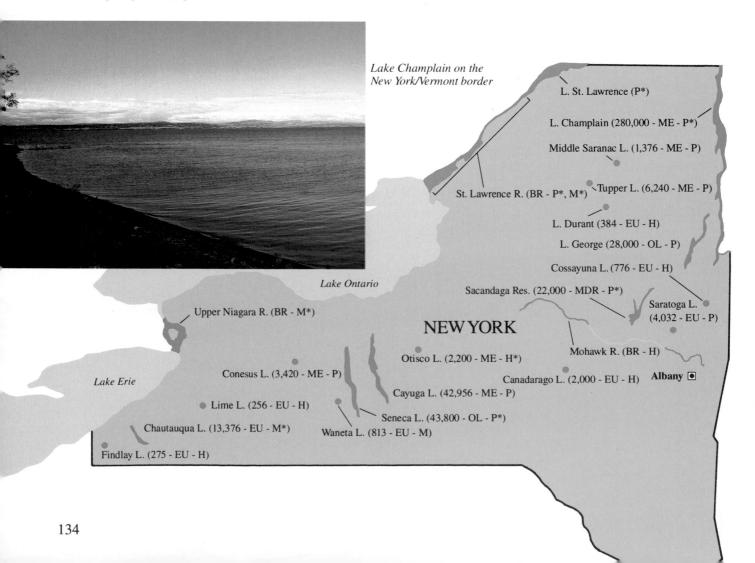

Lake Champlain on the New York/Vermont border

Lake Ontario

Lake Erie

L. St. Lawrence (P*)

L. Champlain (280,000 - ME - P*)

Middle Saranac L. (1,376 - ME - P)

Tupper L. (6,240 - ME - P)

St. Lawrence R. (BR - P*, M*)

L. Durant (384 - EU - H)

L. George (28,000 - OL - P)

Cossayuna L. (776 - EU - H)

Sacandaga Res. (22,000 - MDR - P*)

Saratoga L. (4,032 - EU - P)

Upper Niagara R. (BR - M*)

NEW YORK

Mohawk R. (BR - H)

Otisco L. (2,200 - ME - H*)

Conesus L. (3,420 - ME - P)

Canadarago L. (2,000 - EU - H)

Albany ◉

Cayuga L. (42,956 - ME - P)

Lime L. (256 - EU - H)

Seneca L. (43,800 - OL - P*)

Chautauqua L. (13,376 - EU - M*)

Waneta L. (813 - EU - M)

Findlay L. (275 - EU - H)

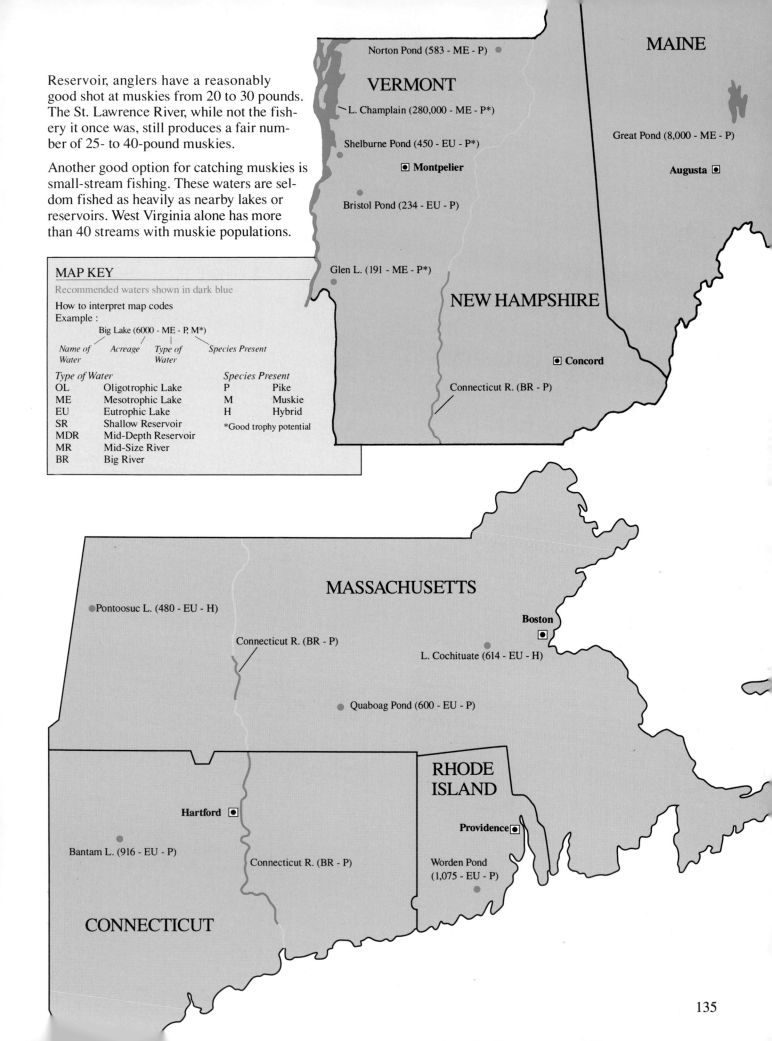

Reservoir, anglers have a reasonably good shot at muskies from 20 to 30 pounds. The St. Lawrence River, while not the fishery it once was, still produces a fair number of 25- to 40-pound muskies.

Another good option for catching muskies is small-stream fishing. These waters are seldom fished as heavily as nearby lakes or reservoirs. West Virginia alone has more than 40 streams with muskie populations.

MAINE

Norton Pond (583 - ME - P)

VERMONT

L. Champlain (280,000 - ME - P*)

Shelburne Pond (450 - EU - P*)

Great Pond (8,000 - ME - P)

⊡ Montpelier

Augusta ⊡

Bristol Pond (234 - EU - P)

MAP KEY

Recommended waters shown in dark blue

How to interpret map codes
Example :

Big Lake (6000 - ME - P, M*)

Name of Water   *Acreage*   *Type of Water*   *Species Present*

Type of Water		*Species Present*	
OL	Oligotrophic Lake	P	Pike
ME	Mesotrophic Lake	M	Muskie
EU	Eutrophic Lake	H	Hybrid
SR	Shallow Reservoir		
MDR	Mid-Depth Reservoir	*Good trophy potential	
MR	Mid-Size River		
BR	Big River		

Glen L. (191 - ME - P*)

NEW HAMPSHIRE

⊡ Concord

Connecticut R. (BR - P)

MASSACHUSETTS

●Pontoosuc L. (480 - EU - H)

Boston
⊡

Connecticut R. (BR - P)

L. Cochituate (614 - EU - H)

Quaboag Pond (600 - EU - P)

RHODE ISLAND

Hartford ⊡

Providence ⊡

Bantam L. (916 - EU - P)

Connecticut R. (BR - P)

Worden Pond
(1,075 - EU - P)

CONNECTICUT

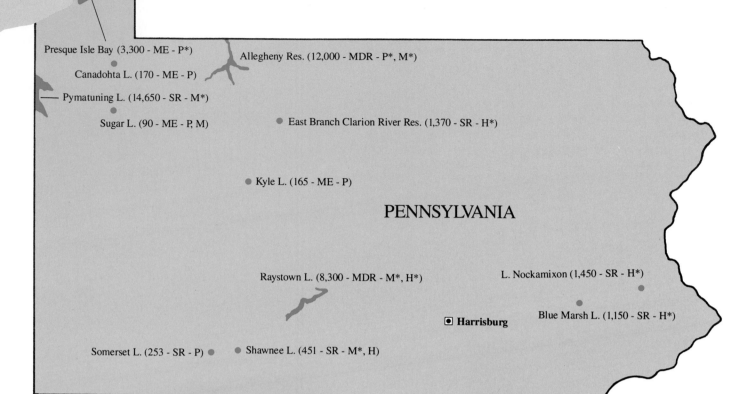

Lake Erie

Presque Isle Bay (3,300 - ME - P*)

Canadohta L. (170 - ME - P)

Pymatuning L. (14,650 - SR - M*)

Sugar L. (90 - ME - P, M)

Allegheny Res. (12,000 - MDR - P*, M*)

East Branch Clarion River Res. (1,370 - SR - H*)

Kyle L. (165 - ME - P)

PENNSYLVANIA

Raystown L. (8,300 - MDR - M*, H*)

L. Nockamixon (1,450 - SR - H*)

⊙ **Harrisburg**

Blue Marsh L. (1,150 - SR - H*)

Somerset L. (253 - SR - P)   Shawnee L. (451 - SR - M*, H)

Delaware River, New Jersey

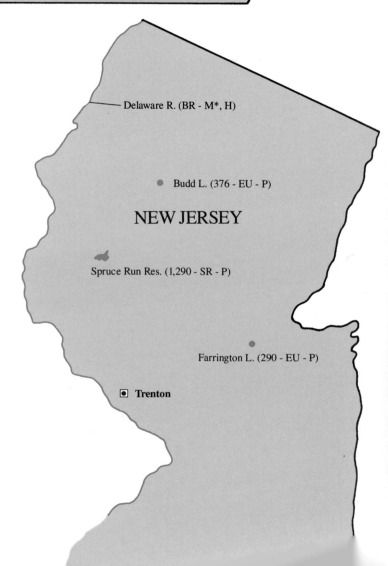

Delaware R. (BR - M*, H)

Budd L. (376 - EU - P)

NEW JERSEY

Spruce Run Res. (1,290 - SR - P)

Farrington L. (290 - EU - P)

⊙ **Trenton**

136

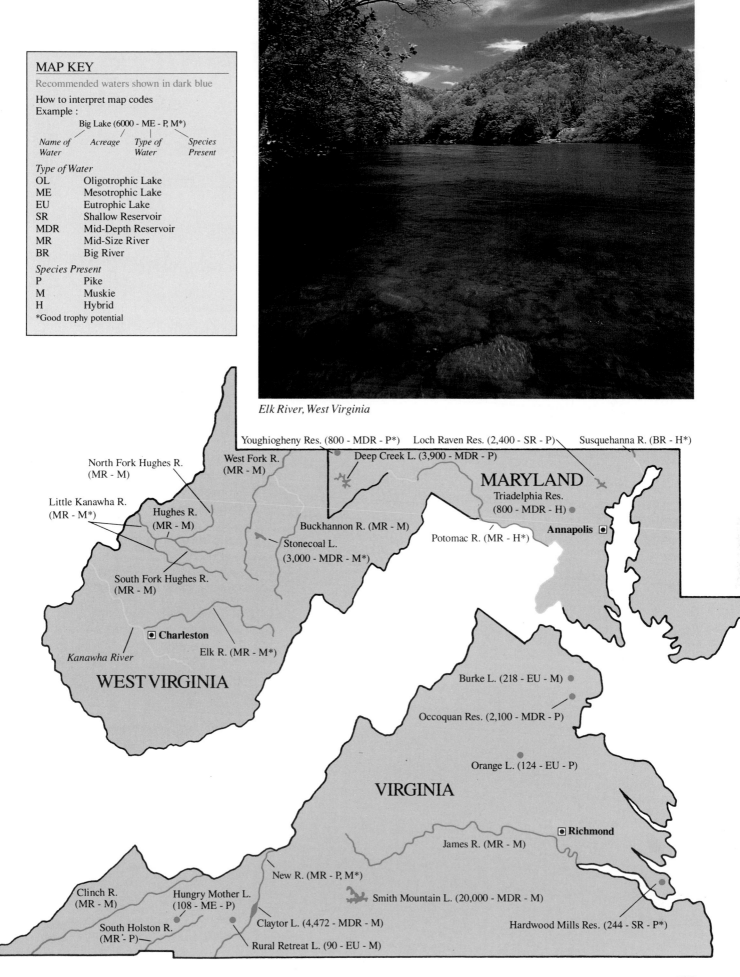

Elk River, West Virginia

Basswood Lake, Minnesota

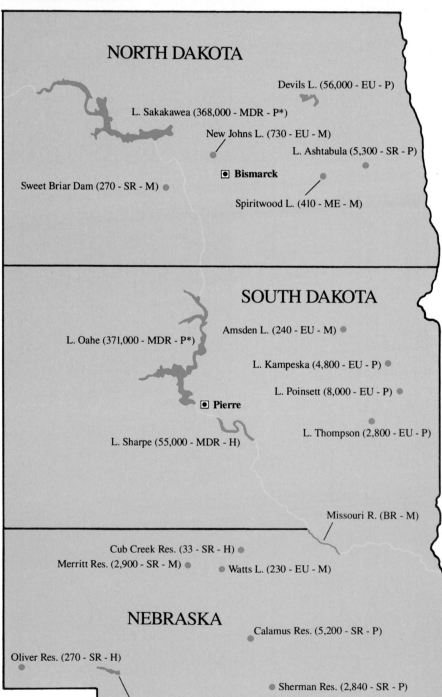

NORTH DAKOTA

Devils L. (56,000 - EU - P)

L. Sakakawea (368,000 - MDR - P*)

New Johns L. (730 - EU - M)

L. Ashtabula (5,300 - SR - P)

⊡ Bismarck

Sweet Briar Dam (270 - SR - M)

Spiritwood L. (410 - ME - M)

SOUTH DAKOTA

Amsden L. (240 - EU - M)

L. Oahe (371,000 - MDR - P*)

L. Kampeska (4,800 - EU - P)

L. Poinsett (8,000 - EU - P)

⊡ Pierre

L. Thompson (2,800 - EU - P)

L. Sharpe (55,000 - MDR - H)

Missouri R. (BR - M)

Cub Creek Res. (33 - SR - H)

Merritt Res. (2,900 - SR - M)

Watts L. (230 - EU - M)

NEBRASKA

Calamus Res. (5,200 - SR - P)

Oliver Res. (270 - SR - H)

Sherman Res. (2,840 - SR - P)

L. McConaughy (30,000 - MDR - H)

⊡ Lincoln

The Midwest

The Midwest is the heart of Esocid country, with an abundance of pike and muskies and more hybrids than any other region. Midwestern states have every conceivable type of pike and muskie water, from small streams to deep oligotrophic lakes to Great Lakes bays and connecting waters.

Pike are native to practically all midwestern waters and are rarely stocked. Muskies originally inhabited a few of the region's large lakes and river systems and have been introduced into hundreds of others. At present, the region has only about ⅕ as much acreage of muskie water (including hybrids) as pike water.

In the early to mid-1900s, the Midwest was known for its trophy pike and muskies. In 1929, Basswood Lake, a large oligotrophic lake on the Minnesota-Canada border, gave up a 45-pound, 12-ounce pike, a world record at the time. From 1939 to 1949, Wisconsin waters yielded 4 world-record muskies, the largest a 69-pound,11-ounce giant caught in the Chippewa Flowage. The others came from large meso lakes. In 1919, Lac Vieux Desert, a meso lake on the Wisconsin-Michigan border, produced the current world-record hybrid, a 51-pound, 3-ouncer.

By the 1960s, pike and muskie populations were

showing the effects of heavy fishing pressure and improved technology. Pike over 25 pounds and muskies over 40 were becoming a rarity.

Today, midwestern waters yield plenty of muskies in the 20- to 30-pound class, with an occasional 35- or 40-pounder. Pike run 2 to 8 pounds in waters that are heavily fished; 5 to 15 with an outside chance for a 20 or 25, where fishing pressure is light. Large natural lakes, big river systems and parts of the Great Lakes have the best big-fish potential.

To restrict the harvest of big muskies, most midwestern states have adopted higher minimum-size limits, often 36 to 40 inches and sometimes as high as 48. Few waters have size limits on pike, but many anglers feel such regulations are badly needed.

Darkhouse spearing (p. 24), which is still allowed in Minnesota, Michigan and South Dakota, accounts for an inordinate number of big pike. The latter two states also allow some spearing of muskies. The topic of spearing generates a tremendous amount of controversy. Opponents call it "dark-ages fish management," while spearers say they have as much right to the fish as anglers do.

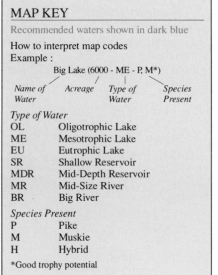

MAP KEY

Recommended waters shown in dark blue

How to interpret map codes
Example :

Big Lake (6000 - ME - P, M*)

| *Name of Water* | *Acreage* | *Type of Water* | *Species Present* |

Type of Water

OL	Oligotrophic Lake
ME	Mesotrophic Lake
EU	Eutrophic Lake
SR	Shallow Reservoir
MDR	Mid-Depth Reservoir
MR	Mid-Size River
BR	Big River

Species Present

P	Pike
M	Muskie
H	Hybrid

*Good trophy potential

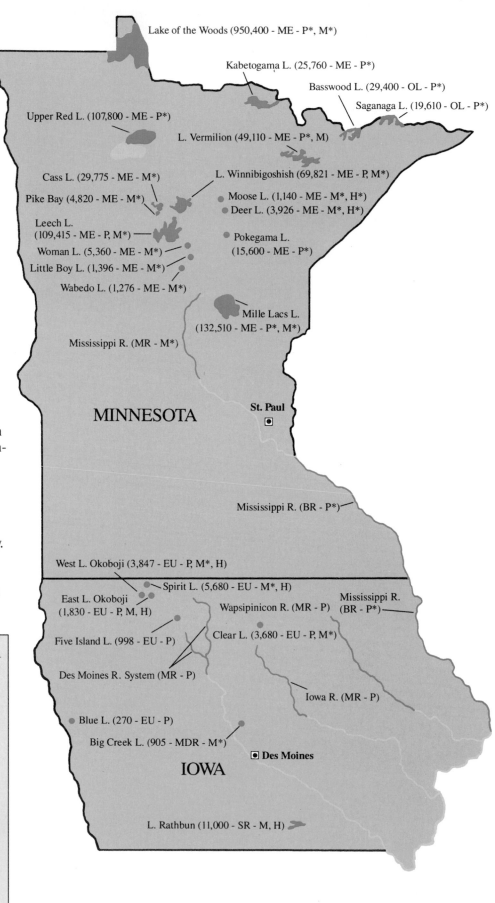

Lake of the Woods (950,400 - ME - P*, M*)

Kabetogama L. (25,760 - ME - P*)

Basswood L. (29,400 - OL - P*)

Saganaga L. (19,610 - OL - P*)

Upper Red L. (107,800 - ME - P*)

L. Vermilion (49,110 - ME - P*, M)

Cass L. (29,775 - ME - M*)

L. Winnibigoshish (69,821 - ME - P, M*)

Pike Bay (4,820 - ME - M*)

Moose L. (1,140 - ME - M*, H*)

Deer L. (3,926 - ME - M*, H*)

Leech L. (109,415 - ME - P, M*)

Pokegama L. (15,600 - ME - P*)

Woman L. (5,360 - ME - M*)

Little Boy L. (1,396 - ME - M*)

Wabedo L. (1,276 - ME - M*)

Mille Lacs L. (132,510 - ME - P*, M*)

Mississippi R. (MR - M*)

MINNESOTA

St. Paul ▣

Mississippi R. (BR - P*)

West L. Okoboji (3,847 - EU - P, M*, H)

Spirit L. (5,680 - EU - M*, H)

East L. Okoboji (1,830 - EU - P, M, H)

Wapsipinicon R. (MR - P)

Mississippi R. (BR - P*)

Five Island L. (998 - EU - P)

Clear L. (3,680 - EU - P, M*)

Des Moines R. System (MR - P)

Iowa R. (MR - P)

Blue L. (270 - EU - P)

Big Creek L. (905 - MDR - M*)

▣ **Des Moines**

IOWA

L. Rathbun (11,000 - SR - M, H)

139

Chippewa Flowage, Wisconsin

MAP KEY

Recommended waters shown in dark blue

How to interpret map codes
Example :

Big Lake (6000 - ME - P, M*)

| *Name of Water* | *Acreage* | *Type of Water* | *Species Present* |

Type of Water

OL	Oligotrophic Lake
ME	Mesotrophic Lake
EU	Eutrophic Lake
SR	Shallow Reservoir
MDR	Mid-Depth Reservoir
MR	Mid-Size River
BR	Big River

Species Present

P	Pike
M	Muskie
H	Hybrid

*Good trophy potential

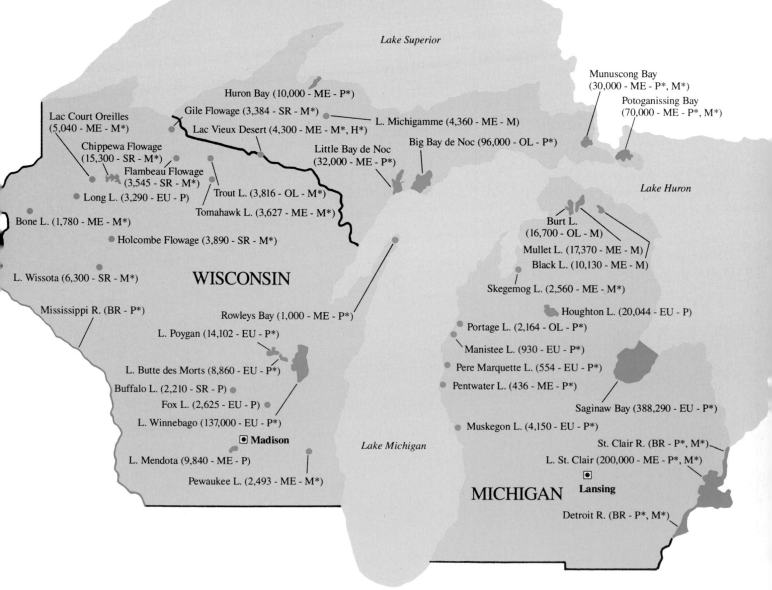

Lake Superior

Munuscong Bay (30,000 - ME - P*, M*)

Potoganissing Bay (70,000 - ME - P*, M*)

Huron Bay (10,000 - ME - P*)

Gile Flowage (3,384 - SR - M*)

Lac Court Oreilles (5,040 - ME - M*)

Lac Vieux Desert (4,300 - ME - M*, H*)

L. Michigamme (4,360 - ME - M)

Big Bay de Noc (96,000 - OL - P*)

Chippewa Flowage (15,300 - SR - M*)

Flambeau Flowage (3,545 - SR - M*)

Little Bay de Noc (32,000 - ME - P*)

Lake Huron

Long L. (3,290 - EU - P)

Trout L. (3,816 - OL - M*)

Tomahawk L. (3,627 - ME - M*)

Bone L. (1,780 - ME - M*)

Burt L. (16,700 - OL - M)

Holcombe Flowage (3,890 - SR - M*)

Mullet L. (17,370 - ME - M)

Black L. (10,130 - ME - M)

Skegemog L. (2,560 - ME - M*)

WISCONSIN

L. Wissota (6,300 - SR - M*)

Houghton L. (20,044 - EU - P)

Mississippi R. (BR - P*)

Rowleys Bay (1,000 - ME - P*)

Portage L. (2,164 - OL - P*)

Manistee L. (930 - EU - P*)

L. Poygan (14,102 - EU - P*)

Pere Marquette L. (554 - EU - P*)

L. Butte des Morts (8,860 - EU - P*)

Pentwater L. (436 - ME - P*)

Buffalo L. (2,210 - SR - P)

Fox L. (2,625 - EU - P)

Saginaw Bay (388,290 - EU - P*)

L. Winnebago (137,000 - EU - P*)

Muskegon L. (4,150 - EU - P*)

◉ **Madison**

Lake Michigan

St. Clair R. (BR - P*, M*)

L. Mendota (9,840 - ME - P)

L. St. Clair (200,000 - ME - P*, M*)

◉
Pewaukee L. (2,493 - ME - M*)

MICHIGAN   **Lansing**

Detroit R. (BR - P*, M*)

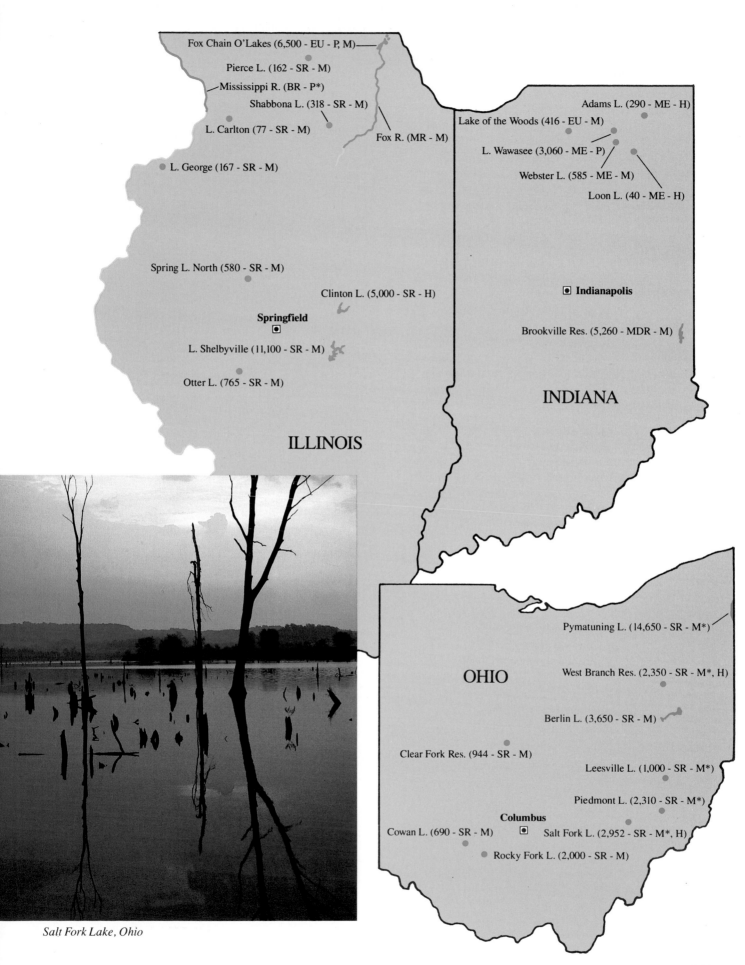

Fox Chain O'Lakes (6,500 - EU - P, M)

Pierce L. (162 - SR - M)

Mississippi R. (BR - P*)

Shabbona L. (318 - SR - M)

L. Carlton (77 - SR - M)

Fox R. (MR - M)

L. George (167 - SR - M)

Spring L. North (580 - SR - M)

Clinton L. (5,000 - SR - H)

Springfield

L. Shelbyville (11,100 - SR - M)

Otter L. (765 - SR - M)

ILLINOIS

Adams L. (290 - ME - H)

Lake of the Woods (416 - EU - M)

L. Wawasee (3,060 - ME - P)

Webster L. (585 - ME - M)

Loon L. (40 - ME - H)

⊡ **Indianapolis**

Brookville Res. (5,260 - MDR - M)

INDIANA

Pymatuning L. (14,650 - SR - M*)

OHIO

West Branch Res. (2,350 - SR - M*, H)

Berlin L. (3,650 - SR - M)

Clear Fork Res. (944 - SR - M)

Leesville L. (1,000 - SR - M*)

Piedmont L. (2,310 - SR - M*)

Columbus
⊡

Cowan L. (690 - SR - M)

Salt Fork L. (2,952 - SR - M*, H)

Rocky Fork L. (2,000 - SR - M)

Salt Fork Lake, Ohio

141

The West

Most of this region is outside the pike's native range, but stocking – much of it illegal – has scattered the fish throughout the West, with the exception of California, Washington and Oregon. The majority of the region's pike water is found in Montana, Idaho, Colorado and New Mexico, although a small number of lakes in Arizona, Utah, Nevada and Wyoming are managed for pike. Tiger muskies have been stocked in a few lakes, mainly in Colorado and Montana. There are no purebred muskies in the region.

The waters stocked with pike vary from deep canyon reservoirs to shallow millponds to big rivers. Pike run 3 to 6 pounds in most western waters; 5 to 10 with an outside chance at a 20, in the better ones. Even bigger pike come from large, deep natural lakes and reservoirs, particularly in Idaho and Montana. In many of these waters, such as Idaho's Coeur d'Alene Lake, pike grow at an astounding rate because of their salmonid diet, reaching weights up to 30 pounds in only 7 years.

Most anglers in this region are trout-oriented; pike see only light fishing pressure, except when they're concentrated in their spawning bays in spring. Then, the most effective method is bobber fishing with dead smelt. Once the water warms, the fish move to deeper weedbeds where anglers casting or trolling with big spoons, spinnerbaits, jigs and minnow plugs make some impressive catches.

Pike management in the West is a controversial topic. In the opinion of many western fisheries managers and fishermen, pike pose a serious threat to existing trout fisheries. They advocate regulations to reduce existing pike populations, explaining why there are very generous limits and no seasons on some of the best pike waters. But others feel that pike provide a tremendous fishing resource and deserve more protection – specifically, regulations to prevent overharvest of trophy pike at spawning time.

☐ States with prime pike and muskie waters

MAP KEY

Recommended waters shown in dark blue

How to interpret map codes
Example :

Big Lake (6000 - ME - P, M*)

Name of Water / *Acreage* / *Type of Water* / *Species Present*

Type of Water
ME   Mesotrophic Lake
EU   Eutrophic Lake
SR   Shallow Reservoir
MDR   Mid-Depth Reservoir
MR   Mid-Size River
BR   Big River

Species Present
P   Pike
H   Hybrid

*Good trophy potential

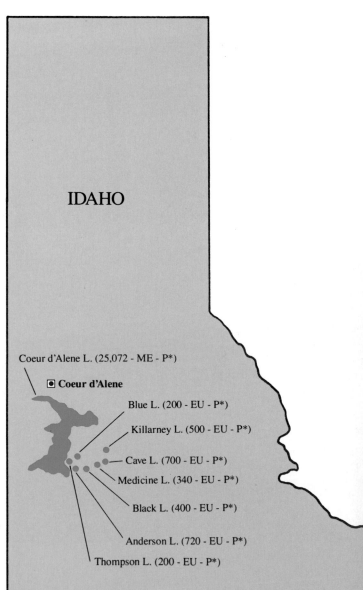

IDAHO

Coeur d'Alene L. (25,072 - ME - P*)

☉ **Coeur d'Alene**

Blue L. (200 - EU - P*)

Killarney L. (500 - EU - P*)

Cave L. (700 - EU - P*)

Medicine L. (340 - EU - P*)

Black L. (400 - EU - P*)

Anderson L. (720 - EU - P*)

Thompson L. (200 - EU - P*)

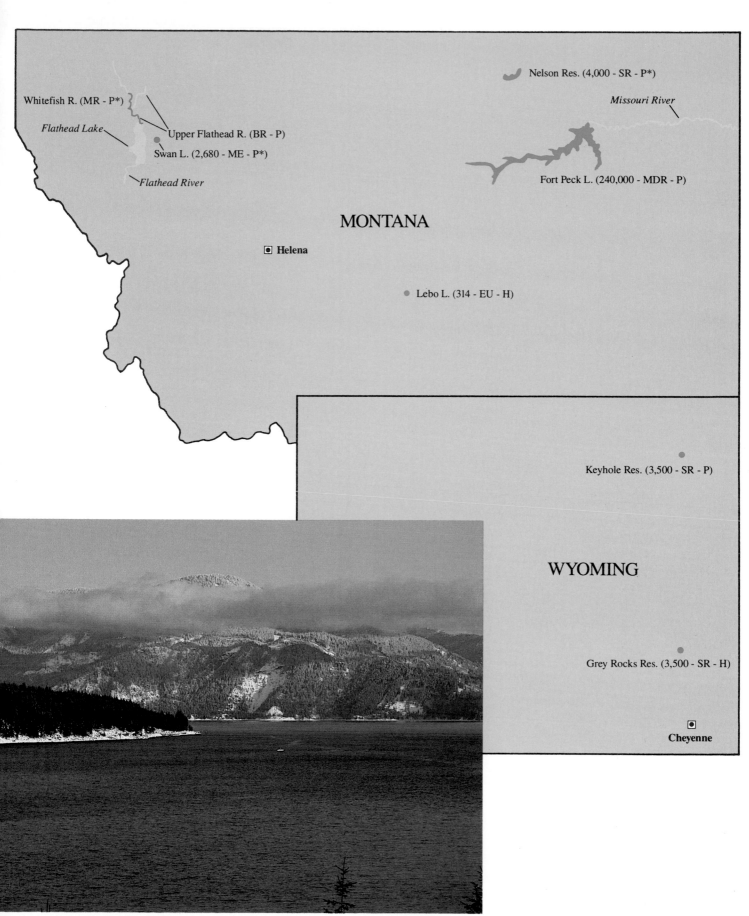

Whitefish R. (MR - P*)

Flathead Lake

Swan L. (2,680 - ME - P*)

Upper Flathead R. (BR - P)

Flathead River

Nelson Res. (4,000 - SR - P*)

Missouri River

Fort Peck L. (240,000 - MDR - P)

MONTANA

◉ **Helena**

● Lebo L. (314 - EU - H)

● Keyhole Res. (3,500 - SR - P)

WYOMING

● Grey Rocks Res. (3,500 - SR - H)

◉
Cheyenne

Coeur d'Alene Lake, Idaho

NEVADA

Bassett L. (80 - SR - P) •

◉
Ely

UTAH

◉ **Salt Lake City**

Green R. (MR - P)

Sevier Bridge Res. (10,900 - SR - P)

• Redmond Res. (160 - SR - P)

ARIZONA

• L. Mary (600 - SR - P)

• • Long L. (270 - SR - P)

Stoneman L. (170 - SR - P)

◉ **Phoenix**

Stoneman Lake, Arizona

MAP KEY

Recommended waters shown in dark blue

How to interpret map codes
Example :

Big Lake (6000 / ME / P. M*)

| Name of Water | Acreage | Type of Water | Species Present |

Type of Water
SR   Shallow Reservoir
MDR   Mid-Depth Reservoir
MR   Mid-Size River
BR   Big River

Species Present
P   Pike
H   Hybrid

*Good trophy potential

Williams Fork Reservoir, Colorado

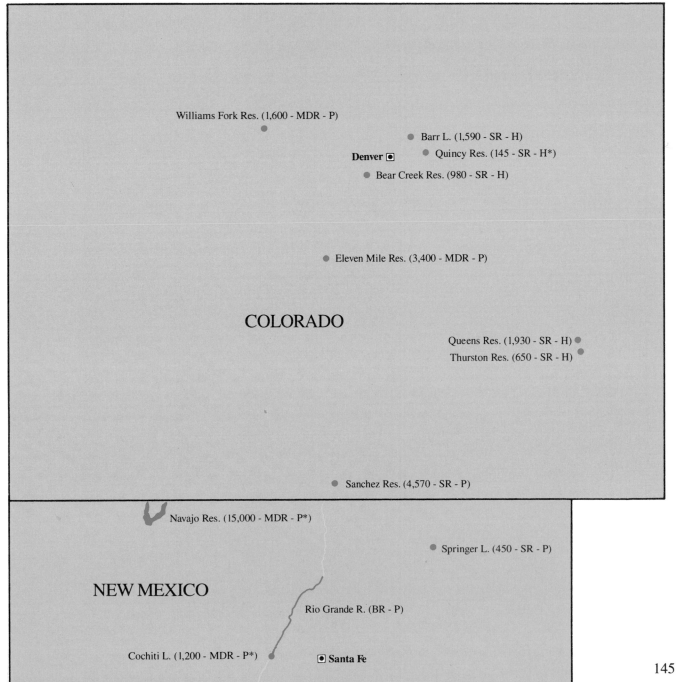

Williams Fork Res. (1,600 - MDR - P)

Barr L. (1,590 - SR - H)

Denver ◙   Quincy Res. (145 - SR - H*)

Bear Creek Res. (980 - SR - H)

Eleven Mile Res. (3,400 - MDR - P)

COLORADO

Queens Res. (1,930 - SR - H)
Thurston Res. (650 - SR - H)

Sanchez Res. (4,570 - SR - P)

Navajo Res. (15,000 - MDR - P*)

Springer L. (450 - SR - P)

NEW MEXICO

Rio Grande R. (BR - P)

Cochiti L. (1,200 - MDR - P*)   ◙ **Santa Fe**

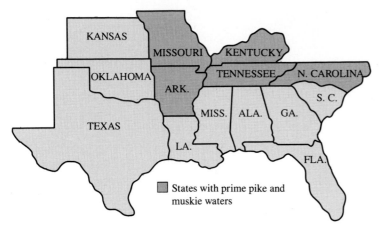

States with prime pike and muskie waters

The South

A few southern states offer quality muskie fishing, but on a very limited scale. The best fisheries are in Missouri and Kentucky; lesser ones in Tennessee and North Carolina. Although muskies reproduce naturally in some waters, most populations are maintained by stocking. Tiger muskies have been planted in several southern states, but the returns have been poor. Most states, with the exception of Arkansas, have discontinued such programs. There is no pike fishing of any consequence in the region.

Mid-depth reservoirs with high shad populations produce the biggest muskies. Dozens in the 20- to 30-pound class are caught each year, and a few 40-pounders have been taken in Kentucky. The fish grow rapidly, sometimes topping the 40-pound mark in only 12 years. Some rivers hold good muskie populations too, but the fish run considerably smaller, averaging from 6 to 12 pounds.

Reservoir fishing peaks in September and October, when cooling water draws the fish onto shallow feeding areas. Drawdowns concentrate the fish on humps and points adjacent to the old river channel, where they're caught on bucktails, buzzbaits

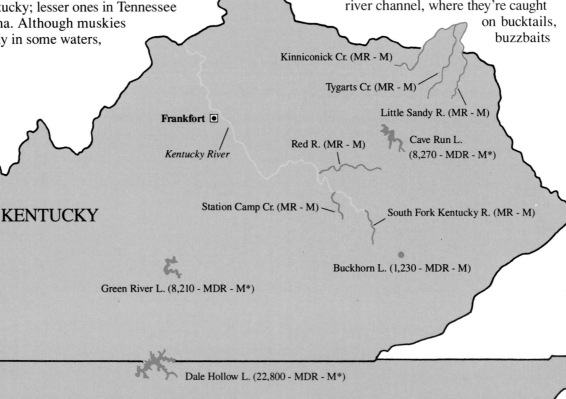

Kinniconick Cr. (MR - M)

Tygarts Cr. (MR - M)

Little Sandy R. (MR - M)

Frankfort ◉

Kentucky River

Red R. (MR - M)

Cave Run L. (8,270 - MDR - M*)

Station Camp Cr. (MR - M)

South Fork Kentucky R. (MR - M)

KENTUCKY

Buckhorn L. (1,230 - MDR - M)

Green River L. (8,210 - MDR - M*)

Dale Hollow L. (22,800 - MDR - M*)

Nolichucky R. (MR - M)

◉ **Nashville**

Obed R. (MR - M)

Emory R. (MR - M)

Caney Fork R. (MR - M)

TENNESSEE

Great Falls Res. (2,270 - MDR - M*)

Woods Res. (3,910 - SR - M)

and jerkbaits. River fishing is best in summer and fall, when low water pulls the fish into deep pools. Productive lures include bucktails, crankbaits and topwaters.

In this bass-fishing hotbed, muskies are of limited interest to most anglers, so even the best waters see only moderate fishing pressure. There is little chance that stocking efforts will be expanded until anglers show more enthusiasm for the program.

Muskie fishing throughout the region is open all year. In most waters, the minimum legal size is 30 inches.

MAP KEY

Recommended waters shown in dark blue

How to interpret map codes
Example :

Big Lake (6000 - ME - P, M*)

Name of Water   *Acreage*   *Type of Water*   *Species Present*

Type of Water		*Species Present*	
SR	Shallow Reservoir	M	Muskie
MDR	Mid-Depth Reservoir	H	Hybrid
MR	Mid-Size River	*Good trophy potential	

Hazel Creek L. (500 - SR - M)

Pony Express L. (250 - SR - M)

MISSOURI

⊙ Jefferson City

Pomme de Terre L. (7,800 - MDR - M*)

Spring R. (MR - H)

L. Hasbaugh (525 - SR - H)

ARKANSAS

⊙ Little Rock

New R. (MR - M)

South Fork New R. (MR - M)

⊙ Boone   *North Fork New River*

Nolichucky R. (MR - M)

NORTH CAROLINA

North Toe River
Cane River

French Broad R. (MR - M)

L. Adger (500 - SR - M*)

Fontana Res. (11,000 - MDR - M)

Little Tennessee R. (MR - M*)

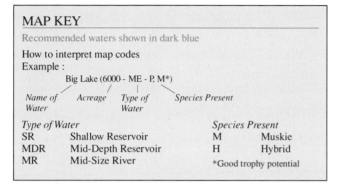

Dale Hollow Lake, Tennessee

Alaska & the Yukon

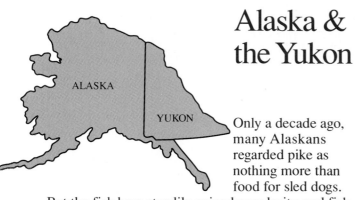

Only a decade ago, many Alaskans regarded pike as nothing more than food for sled dogs.

But the fish have steadily gained popularity, and fishing pressure has increased so much that some waters are now being overharvested. In fact, size limits have been established on certain waters, and others have been closed to fishing in winter.

Northern pike are native to Alaska and the Yukon and are the only Esocids present. Found throughout the region, with the exception of a few watersheds in south-central and southeastern Alaska, pike thrive in slow, meandering, weedy rivers, sloughs connected to them and warm, shallow bays of deep lakes.

Despite their slow growth rate, pike in this region reach surprisingly large sizes, especially in waters with plenty of high-fat forage such as whitefish and trout. Pike commonly live 20 to 25 years and reach weights of 15 to 25 pounds. The biggest fish, including a few over 35 pounds, come from fly-in

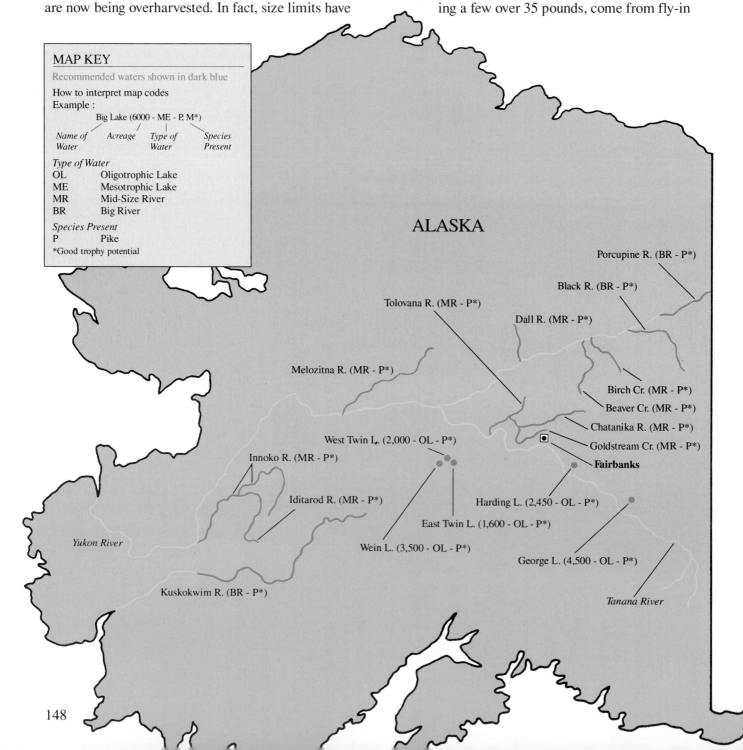

MAP KEY

Recommended waters shown in dark blue

How to interpret map codes
Example :

Big Lake (6000 - ME - P, M*)

| Name of Water | Acreage | Type of Water | Species Present |

Type of Water
OL   Oligotrophic Lake
ME   Mesotrophic Lake
MR   Mid-Size River
BR   Big River

Species Present
P   Pike
*Good trophy potential

ALASKA

Porcupine R. (BR - P*)

Black R. (BR - P*)

Tolovana R. (MR - P*)

Dall R. (MR - P*)

Melozitna R. (MR - P*)

Birch Cr. (MR - P*)

Beaver Cr. (MR - P*)

Chatanika R. (MR - P*)

West Twin L. (2,000 - OL - P*)

Goldstream Cr. (MR - P*)

Innoko R. (MR - P*)

Fairbanks

Iditarod R. (MR - P*)

Harding L. (2,450 - OL - P*)

East Twin L. (1,600 - OL - P*)

Yukon River

Wein L. (3,500 - OL - P*)

George L. (4,500 - OL - P*)

Kuskokwim R. (BR - P*)

Tanana River

lakes or out-of-the-way sloughs, particularly those in the Yukon River drainage. Easily accessible waters are fished heavily, but still produce lots of pike in the 5- to 10-pound range.

Fishing is best just after ice-out, when pike move into shallow bays and sloughs to spawn. Most anglers use artificials; live baitfish are banned throughout the region.

Spoons are most popular, but spinnerbaits, jerkbaits and topwaters also work well. Another effective technique is fly fishing with

divers. Once the water warms in summer, pike retreat to deeper, cooler water where they're difficult to find.

Local anglers do a fair amount of tip-up fishing in winter, when they can easily reach remote waters by snowmobile. Swedish hooks (p. 127) with dead bait, such as herring or smelt, produce good numbers of hefty pike.

Most of this region is roadless wilderness with few accommodations for anglers, but those interested in a trophy-pike fishing adventure can contact the Fairbanks Chamber of Commerce or the tourism office in Whitehorse for recommendations on outfitters and flying services.

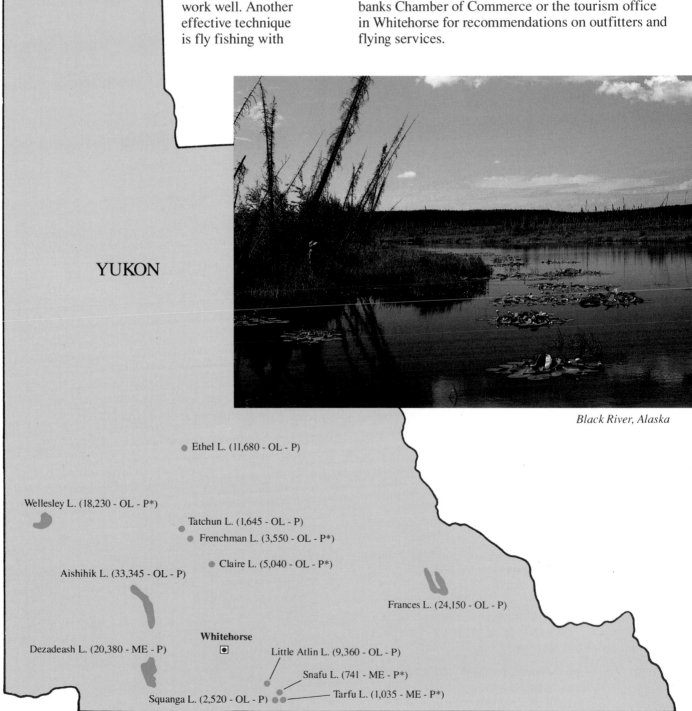

Black River, Alaska

YUKON

Ethel L. (11,680 - OL - P)

Wellesley L. (18,230 - OL - P*)

Tatchun L. (1,645 - OL - P)

Frenchman L. (3,550 - OL - P*)

Claire L. (5,040 - OL - P*)

Aishihik L. (33,345 - OL - P)

Frances L. (24,150 - OL - P)

Whitehorse

Dezadeash L. (20,380 - ME - P)

Little Atlin L. (9,360 - OL - P)

Snafu L. (741 - ME - P*)

Squanga L. (2,520 - OL - P)

Tarfu L. (1,035 - ME - P*)

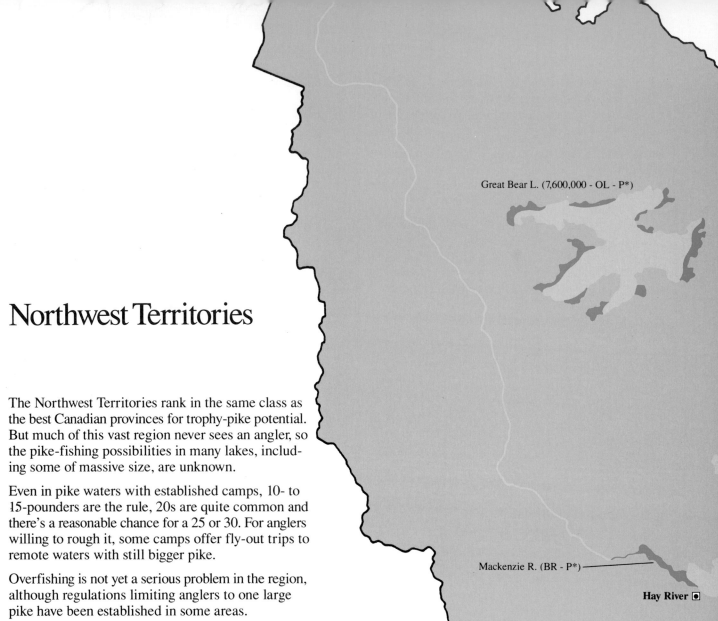

Great Bear L. (7,600,000 - OL - P*)

Mackenzie R. (BR - P*) ————————————

Hay River ◉

Northwest Territories

The Northwest Territories rank in the same class as the best Canadian provinces for trophy-pike potential. But much of this vast region never sees an angler, so the pike-fishing possibilities in many lakes, including some of massive size, are unknown.

Even in pike waters with established camps, 10- to 15-pounders are the rule, 20s are quite common and there's a reasonable chance for a 25 or 30. For anglers willing to rough it, some camps offer fly-out trips to remote waters with still bigger pike.

Overfishing is not yet a serious problem in the region, although regulations limiting anglers to one large pike have been established in some areas.

Pike are found mainly to the south of a diagonal line connecting the northwest and southeast corners of the Territories. The best pike waters include shallow lakes, weedy bays of deeper lakes, and large rivers, especially where they widen out into lakes. The entire region is out of the muskies' range.

Most pike lakes in this region remain icebound 7 to 8 months out of the year. Lodges generally open in mid-June and close in mid-September. Fishing is easiest in the weeks following ice-out, when pike concentrate in the back ends of bays and around inlet streams. But some areas are closed to fishing at this time to protect the spawners. The surface water stays cool through the summer, so the fish continue to bite, although they're not as concentrated as they were earlier. The natives do some spearing and ice fishing for pike, but severe winter weather keeps these activities to a minimum.

The traditional pike-fishing method is casting with spoons, particularly weedless models tipped with a pork strip. But practically any good-sized lure will work; the fish aren't as fussy as their southern relatives. Live bait is illegal throughout the Territories.

For information on fishing in the Northwest Territories, contact the tourism office in Yellowknife. They will supply names of lodges, mostly in the Hay River area, that specialize in pike fishing and a list of charter services that will fly you to waters that rarely see an angler.

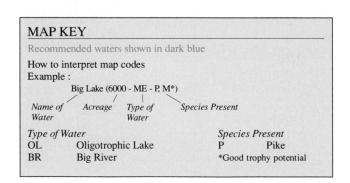

MAP KEY

Recommended waters shown in dark blue

How to interpret map codes
Example :

Big Lake (6000 - ME - P, M*)

Name of Water | Acreage | Type of Water | Species Present

Type of Water		Species Present	
OL	Oligotrophic Lake	P	Pike
BR	Big River	*Good trophy potential	

150

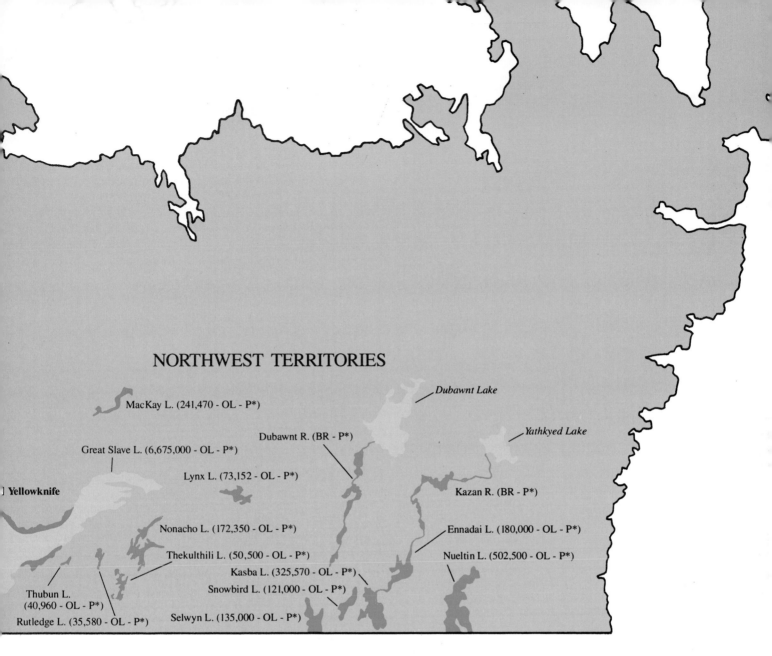

NORTHWEST TERRITORIES

MacKay L. (241,470 - OL - P*)

Dubawnt Lake

Dubawnt R. (BR - P*)

Yathkyed Lake

Great Slave L. (6,675,000 - OL - P*)

] Yellowknife

Lynx L. (73,152 - OL - P*)

Kazan R. (BR - P*)

Nonacho L. (172,350 - OL - P*)

Ennadai L. (180,000 - OL - P*)

Thekulthili L. (50,500 - OL - P*)

Nueltin L. (502,500 - OL - P*)

Kasba L. (325,570 - OL - P*)

Thubun L.
(40,960 - OL - P*)

Snowbird L. (121,000 - OL - P*)

Rutledge L. (35,580 - OL - P*)

Selwyn L. (135,000 - OL - P*)

Nueltin Lake, Northwest Territories

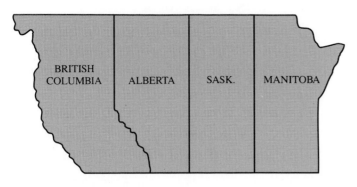

Western Canada

This region is famed for its huge pike. In fact, many consider northern Saskatchewan the best trophy-pike fishing region in North America. No muskies or hybrids are found in western Canada.

Pike abound throughout most of Alberta, Saskatchewan and Manitoba. They're not as widespread in British Columbia, inhabiting only the northeastern and north-central parts of the province.

Easily accessible waters generally produce pike in the 4- to 8-pound range. The big pike come from fly-in lakes, mainly in the northern part of the region. Here, 20- to 25-pounders are commonplace, and it takes a 30-pounder to cause much of a stir. Pike topping the 40-pound mark have been reported, but most of these fish are never officially weighed because of the remote location of the camps.

Most good pike lakes remain icebound until mid to late May. Then, the fish move into shallow bays or concentrate around inlets where anglers casting spoons enjoy fast action. Fall is the time for the real

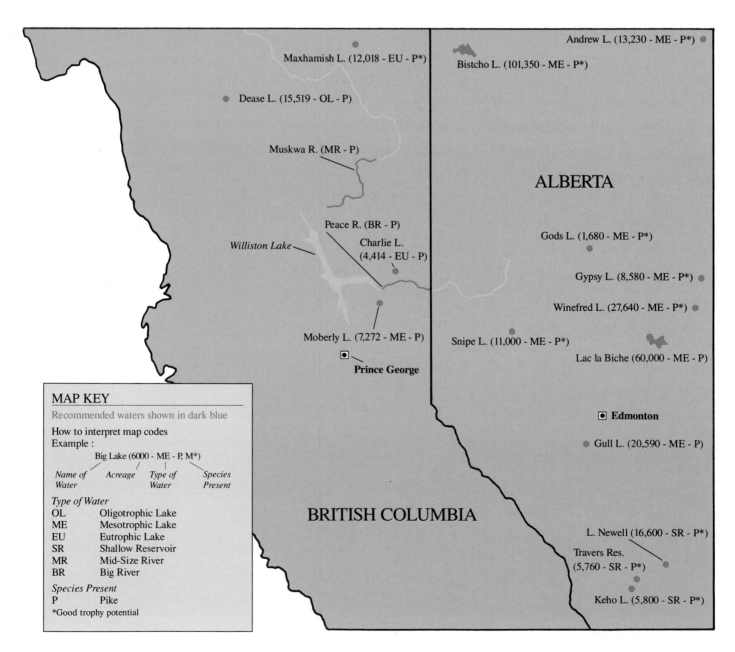

Maxhamish L. (12,018 - EU - P*)
Andrew L. (13,230 - ME - P*)
Bistcho L. (101,350 - ME - P*)
Dease L. (15,519 - OL - P)
Muskwa R. (MR - P)

ALBERTA

Peace R. (BR - P)
Williston Lake
Charlie L. (4,414 - EU - P)
Gods L. (1,680 - ME - P*)
Gypsy L. (8,580 - ME - P*)
Winefred L. (27,640 - ME - P*)
Moberly L. (7,272 - ME - P)
Snipe L. (11,000 - ME - P*)
☐ **Prince George**
Lac la Biche (60,000 - ME - P)

☐ **Edmonton**
● Gull L. (20,590 - ME - P)

BRITISH COLUMBIA

L. Newell (16,600 - SR - P*)
Travers Res. (5,760 - SR - P*)
Keho L. (5,800 - SR - P*)

MAP KEY
Recommended waters shown in dark blue

How to interpret map codes
Example :

Big Lake (6000 - ME - P, M*)

Name of Water / *Acreage* / *Type of Water* / *Species Present*

Type of Water
OL   Oligotrophic Lake
ME   Mesotrophic Lake
EU   Eutrophic Lake
SR   Shallow Reservoir
MR   Mid-Size River
BR   Big River

Species Present
P   Pike
*Good trophy potential

trophies. Beginning in September, you'll find big pike on rocky main-lake humps and points. Work depths of 15 to 20 feet with deep-running plugs or jerkbaits. Not much ice fishing is done because of the harsh winter weather, but those willing to brave the elements have good luck with tip-ups and dead bait in the same spots as in fall.

Even though this region has a staggering number of lakes and relatively few anglers, overfishing is a major concern. Pike in these infertile waters grow very slowly, so it doesn't take much fishing pressure to cause problems. Many lakes are now managed for trophy fishing. A common regulation is one fish over a given size, usually about 34 inches.

Camp operators may impose further restrictions, with some allowing only catch-and-release fishing.

Reindeer Lake on the Saskatchewan/Manitoba border

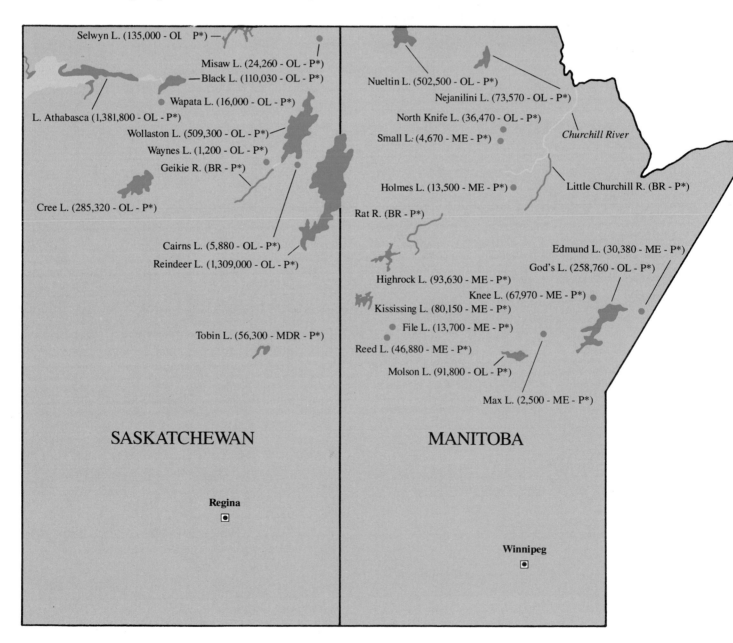

Selwyn L. (135,000 - OL   P*) —
Misaw L. (24,260 - OL - P*)
—Black L. (110,030 - OL - P*)
Wapata L. (16,000 - OL - P*)
L. Athabasca (1,381,800 - OL - P*)
Wollaston L. (509,300 - OL - P*)
Waynes L. (1,200 - OL - P*)
Geikie R. (BR - P*)
Cree L. (285,320 - OL - P*)
Cairns L. (5,880 - OL - P*)
Reindeer L. (1,309,000 - OL - P*)
Tobin L. (56,300 - MDR - P*)

Nueltin L. (502,500 - OL - P*)
Nejanilini L. (73,570 - OL - P*)
North Knife L. (36,470 - OL - P*)
Small L. (4,670 - ME - P*)
Holmes L. (13,500 - ME - P*)
Churchill River
Little Churchill R. (BR - P*)
Rat R. (BR - P*)
Edmund L. (30,380 - ME - P*)
God's L. (258,760 - OL - P*)
Highrock L. (93,630 - ME - P*)
Knee L. (67,970 - ME - P*)
Kississing L. (80,150 - ME - P*)
File L. (13,700 - ME - P*)
Reed L. (46,880 - ME - P*)
Molson L. (91,800 - OL - P*)
Max L. (2,500 - ME - P*)

SASKATCHEWAN

MANITOBA

Regina
◉

Winnipeg
◉

Hudson Bay

ONTARIO

Attawapiskat R. (BR - P*)

Little Vermilion L. (13,927 - OL - P*)

Nungesser L. (18,674 - OL - P*)

Pakwash L. (24,278 - OL - P*)

Albany R. (BR - P*)

L. St. Joseph (127,300 - MDR - P*)   L. Abitibi (223,040 - ME - P*)

Lac Seul (320,000 - MDR - P*, M*)

Upper Twin L. (4,184 - ME - P*)

Eagle L. (68,427 - ME - M*)   L. Nipigon (1,107,000 - OL - P*)

Wabigoon L. (24,520 - EU - M*)

Dryberry L. (26,940 - OL - M*)

Rowan L. (13,500 - OL - M*)   Batchawana Bay (30,000 - ME - P*)

Basswood L.
(29,400 - OL - P*)   L. Nipissing (211,200 - ME - P*, M*)   St. Lawrence R. (BR - P*, M*)

Pipestone L. (9,614 - OL - M*)   French R. (BR - P*, M*)

Saganaga L. (19,610 - OL - P*)   North Channel   L. Nosbonsing (4,200 - EU - M*)
(OL - P*, M*)

Lake of the Woods
(950,400 - ME - P*, M*)   *Lake Superior*   Manitouwabing L. (3,088 - ME - P*)

Moira L. (2,050 - EU - M*)

Rice L. (24,750 - EU - M)

Lake Huron

Georgian Bay   L. Scugog
(15,750 - EU - M)   *Lake Ontario*

Lake Michigan

MICH.   **Toronto**

Georgian Bay
North Shore
(OL - P*, M*)   Niagara R.
(BR - M*)

St. Clair R. (BR - P*, M*)

L. St. Clair
(200,000 - ME - P*, M*)   *Lake Erie*

Detroit R. (BR - P*, M*)

LABR.

NEWF.

QUEBEC

ONTARIO

N. B.   N. S.

☐ Provinces with prime pike and
muskie waters

Eastern Canada

Most muskie hunters agree that no other region can
equal eastern Canada for quality muskie fishing. The
region also produces plenty of good-sized pike, although the chances for a real trophy are greater in
western Canada. A few naturally occurring hybrids
are found in the southern part of the region, wherever
muskies are common. Parts of eastern Canada, including Nova Scotia, Newfoundland and most of
New Brunswick, have no Esocids.

The top muskie waters are the natural lakes of northwestern Ontario, widenings of the St. Lawrence River,
and the north shore of Georgian Bay on Lake Huron.
These areas routinely produce muskies in the 25- to
45-pound class. The Canadian-record muskie, a 65-
pounder, was caught in Blackstone Harbor, where the
Moon River empties into Georgian Bay. Of course,
the St. Lawrence River, where it forms the New York-
Ontario boundary, yielded the current world-record
muskie (p. 134).

You can find pike in the 5- to 10-pound class
throughout most of the region. But for bigger ones,
concentrate on large river systems; bays of the Great

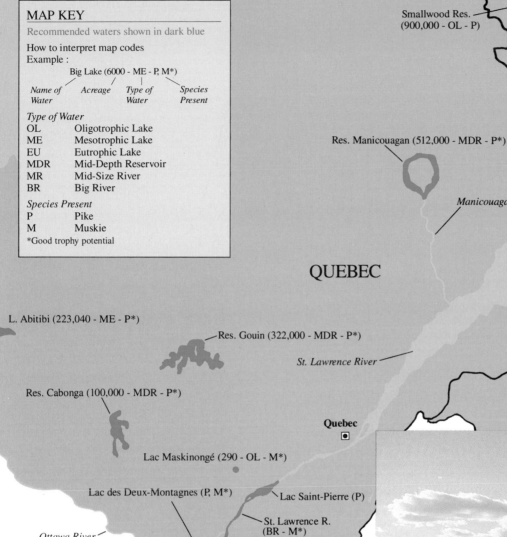

Smallwood Res.
(900,000 - OL - P)

Ossokmanuan L.
(86,500 - OL - P)

LABRADOR

Atikonak R. (MR - P)

Res. Manicouagan (512,000 - MDR - P*)

Manicouagan River

QUEBEC

L. Abitibi (223,040 - ME - P*)

Res. Gouin (322,000 - MDR - P*)

St. Lawrence River

Res. Cabonga (100,000 - MDR - P*)

Quebec

Lac Maskinongé (290 - OL - M*)

Lac des Deux-Montagnes (P, M*)

Lac Saint-Pierre (P)

St. Lawrence R.
(BR - M*)

Ottawa River

Montreal

Lac Saint-Francois (P, M*)

Lac Saint-Louis (P, M*)

MAP KEY

Recommended waters shown in dark blue

How to interpret map codes
Example :

Big Lake (6000 - ME - P, M*)

Name of Water — *Acreage* — *Type of Water* — *Species Present*

Type of Water

OL	Oligotrophic Lake
ME	Mesotrophic Lake
EU	Eutrophic Lake
MDR	Mid-Depth Reservoir
MR	Mid-Size River
BR	Big River

Species Present

P	Pike
M	Muskie

*Good trophy potential

Lakes, particularly the north shore of Georgian Bay; remote natural lakes, such as those in central and northwestern Ontario; and large reservoirs in central Quebec. In 1890, Quebec's Lake Tschotogama produced a 49-pound pike, which was never officially recognized, but may well be the largest ever taken in North America.

With the exception of Ontario, the region sees only light fishing pressure on pike and muskies. Ontario has recently established size restrictions to prevent further overharvest of large pike. The minimum-size limit for muskies has been increased on many waters and the opener delayed to protect spawners.

Another recent change in parts of Ontario is the prohibition of smelt (either live or dead) as bait. The law is intended to prevent smelt, which prey on game-fish fry, from becoming established in more waters than they already are.

French River, Ontario

Index

Cy DeCosse Incorporated offers
Hunting & Fishing Products at
special subscriber discounts.
For information write:

Hunting & Fishing Products
5900 Green Oak Drive
Minnetonka, MN 55343